METROPOLITAN
JEWELRY

METROPOLITAN JEWELRY

Text by
SOPHIE McCONNELL

Design by
ALVIN GROSSMAN

THE METROPOLITAN MUSEUM OF ART, NEW YORK

A BULFINCH PRESS BOOK/LITTLE, BROWN AND COMPANY
BOSTON · TORONTO · LONDON

Copyright © 1991 by The Metropolitan
Museum of Art

First Edition

Library of Congress Cataloging in Publication Data

Metropolitan Museum of Art (New York, N.Y.)
 Metropolitan jewelry :
 text by Sophie McConnell;
 design by Alvin Grossman.
   p. cm.
 ISBN 0-87099-616-9. — ISBN 0-87099-617-7
   (pbk.). — ISBN 0-8212-1877-8 (Bulfinch)
 1. Jewelry — New York (N.Y.) — Catalogs.
 2. Metropolitan Museum of Art
   (New York, N.Y.) — Catalogs.
 I. McConnell, Sophie. II. Title.
 NK7302.N5M486 1991   91-18298
 739.27′074′7471 — dc20   CIP

Produced by The Metropolitan Museum
 of Art, New York
John O'Neill, Editor in Chief
Barbara Burn, Project Supervisor
Alvin Grossman, Designer
Peter Antony, Production

Published by The Metropolitan Museum
 of Art and Bulfinch Press

Bulfinch Press is an imprint and trademark
 of Little, Brown and Company (Inc.)
Published simultaneously in Canada by
 Little, Brown & Company (Canada)
 Limited

The photographs in this volume were
taken by the Photograph Studio of The
Metropolitan Museum of Art, with the
exception of those on pages 33, 38, 88, and
102, which were taken by Schecter Lee.

Composition by Typographic Images,
 New York
Printed and bound by Arnoldo Mondadori
 Editore S.p.A., Verona, Italy

ENDPAPERS **Bracelet of Ring Beads.** Beautifully crafted during the nineteenth century B.C., with many small beads of gold, carnelian, and turquoise together with six large gold spacer beads, this handsome Egyptian bracelet is one of a pair found with the treasure of Princess Sithathoryunet, who may have been the daughter of Pharaoh Senwosret II. The cache of her jewelry included some of the finest pieces surviving from the Middle Kingdom, a period unsurpassed for its elegance and deft workmanship. The use of paste with real gemstones is not unusual in Egyptian jewelry, since the colors, not the materials, were thought to be most significant. The clasps are inlaid with carnelian and blue and green (now white) paste that form the cartouche of Senwosret II's grandson, Amenemhat III, into whose reign the princess survived.

HALF TITLE PAGE **Francesco d'Este** (detail) by Rogier van der Weyden. See page 103.

FRONTISPIECE **Portrait of a Noblewoman** (detail) by unknown sixteenth-century British painter. See page 42.

TITLE PAGE **Bracelet.** Designed and made in Constantinople during the second half of the sixth century or the early seventh, this sumptuous bracelet is one of a number of pieces from the same treasure said to have been found near Assiut in upper Egypt on the eastern bank of the Nile. By the sixth century Constantinople had become the medieval world's leading center for jewelry production. The prestige of its jewelers is attested to by the fact that many examples of their work have been found in areas outside the Byzantine Empire. This bracelet's opulent decoration indicates that it was designed for a woman of great wealth. The wide gold hoop is embellished with strings of pearls and gold beads that frame sapphires and emerald-green plasmas. A hinged central mount is set with a large oval sapphire and surrounded by more pearls. The stones have been polished, but they retain their irregular shape. Jewelry such as this was especially favored by the Byzantine aristocracy and is often represented in the brilliant mosaics that depict the imperial court.

OPPOSITE **Saint Eligius.** Tradition holds that this painting by Petrus Christus (Flemish, act. 1444–73) was commissioned by the Antwerp goldsmiths' guild to help promote their trade. Born in 588, Saint Eligius first worked as a metalsmith, became a saintly bishop of great fame, and after his death was chosen to be the patron saint of goldsmiths and other workers in metal. This intriguing painting provides us with a wealth of knowledge about fifteenth-century goldsmiths. Depicted here as a craftsman, the saint prepares to weigh a ring that the elegant couple will use at their wedding. Behind him is a display of both finished work and raw materials. Rings are stored in a black box; some are plain gold bands, and others are set with one or two cabochon gems. In an envelope beside the box there are unset stones of great and gleaming variety, and behind them is a branch of unworked red coral. An envelope of pearls lies to the left. Hanging on the wall are three brooches, one not unlike that worn on the young man's hat. Draped from the upper shelf is a strand of unstrung beads. In addition to the jewelry we see displayed other objects of the goldsmith's art: glass containers with finely wrought gold fittings. Coins on the table remind us of Saint Eligius's early career as a coiner to Clotaire II, king of the Franks.

PAGE 6 **Saint Eligius** (detail) by Petrus Christus. See page 5.

Introduction

Personal adornment may well have been our earliest art form. Since we first created ornaments of shells and bones, more than 20,000 years ago, we have found countless beautiful and ingenious ways to advance the art. The splendor of gold, the allure of glittering stones, the perfection of pearls, each has worked its magic on virtually every culture throughout history.

The Chinese have produced wonderful objects of carved jade for 5,000 years. In the Americas Precolumbian jewelers, working over the centuries in gold and stone, produced distinctive pieces of great beauty and power. The many cultures of Africa have also made extraordinary objects, using methods ranging from lost-wax casting to the intricate stringing of trade beads.

The oldest piece of jewelry shown in this book is a Sumerian chaplet, a 4,500-year-old wreath of lapis lazuli and carnelian beads with gold-leaf pendants. This splendid object not only demonstrates the skill and artistry of early jewelers, but it also provides evidence of the early existence of trade in precious materials from widespread sources. During this same period the Egyptians began to develop forms of jewelry that would eventually use a full range of materials, from precious gold and semiprecious stones to faience and glass. From the seventh through the fifth century B.C., Etruscan goldsmiths perfected the delicate art of granulation, using a process so sophisticated that it could not be duplicated until this century. The Greeks deftly crafted gold to depict their gods and myths in pieces of jewelry. The Romans excelled at the art of cameo carving, using multicolored stones to represent their emperors as gods. Byzantine jewelers employed stones and enamel in many colors to opulent effect, a practice carried on by Islamic jewelers who followed.

To make wealth transportable during the chaotic Migration Period, it was converted into jewelry; particularly striking are inventive combinations of gold and garnet. The medieval jeweler made secular pieces, but he also used his skills to create magnificent ecclesiastical objects. The arts were transformed during the Renaissance, and intricately imaginative jewels, akin to miniature sculptures, were designed and produced. In the seventeenth century the watchcase provided a new vehicle for exquisite enamel work. Glittering jewelry, from faceted precious stones to faceted steel, became fashionable during the eighteenth century. The eclectic nineteenth saw the revival of earlier styles: Neoclassicism inspired a taste for cameos, while the Arts and Crafts Movement and Art Nouveau kindled renewed interest in the art of enameling.

Although a piece of jewelry may be magnificent in itself, it is always designed to be worn, and, fortunately, we can see jewelry in its proper context in many works of art. Paintings and sculpture, ceramics and drawings enable us to study forms of adornment as they have been portrayed by artists throughout history.

In the fourth century B.C. an Italic sculptor depicted a woman wearing a necklace of bullae, and years later, in nineteenth-century France, Ingres painted a princess wearing the same type of gold pendant. In a nineteenth-century portrait on silk, a Chinese emperor wears a necklace with coral beads; an American child of the same century wears a coral necklace in a portrait painted by Ammi Phillips. Without such works to show us how, and by whom, jewelry was actually worn, our knowledge of the art would be greatly diminished.

Jewelry has not always been worn for its beauty alone. There are, in fact, varied and complex motives behind personal adornment. For thousands of years people have worn jewels for their perceived amuletic value, a practice that continues today. In Egypt some of the most beautiful pieces of jewelry were made as funerary objects, never to be worn by the living. Functional items, such as buckles and clasps, have been so elaborately ornamented that they can certainly be viewed as jewelry. Sovereigns in Europe have long worn jewels to display wealth and power, and many a king has pawned his jewels to finance a war or salvage a bankrupt treasury.

A note of caution: in most cases we can only speculate about the exact identity of the stones and materials represented in the paintings and sculptures reproduced in this book. In some instances, the jewelry depicted survives today or has been documented in inventories and sales records. Generally, however, we must depend on our knowledge of materials in use at the time the work of art was made.

The ancient practice of foiling makes the identification of gemstones quite difficult. The technique of placing thin, colored foil beneath a gem to change its color or enhance its appearance was used intentionally to deceive the viewer. The jewelry rendered in a painting may be beguiling in every sense of the word. Consequently, when the text describes a "ruby" in a painting, for example, it must be read in light of this caveat.

I am immensely grateful for the help I have received from a number of people: Barbara Burn for believing in the book from the beginning and for giving it shape; Clare Le Corbeiller and Clare Vincent for sharing their vast knowledge; the many other curators who gave their help, including Jane Adlin, Dorothea Arnold, Joan Aruz, Kay Bearman, Barbara Boehm, Katharine Brown, Janet Byrne, Kate Ezra, Julie Jones, Carolyn Kane, Steve Kossak, Joan Mertens, Linda Wolk-Simon, and Masako Watanabe; the librarians Deanna Cross, Pat Coman, and Peter Blank; Dorothy Kellett, who broke the ice; Al Grossman, whose erudition is as impressive as his design; Peter Antony, the production maven; my mother, Evelyn Sweetman, for her aesthetic sense; and Malcolm McConnell, whose love of knowledge is more precious than jewels.

Sophie McConnell

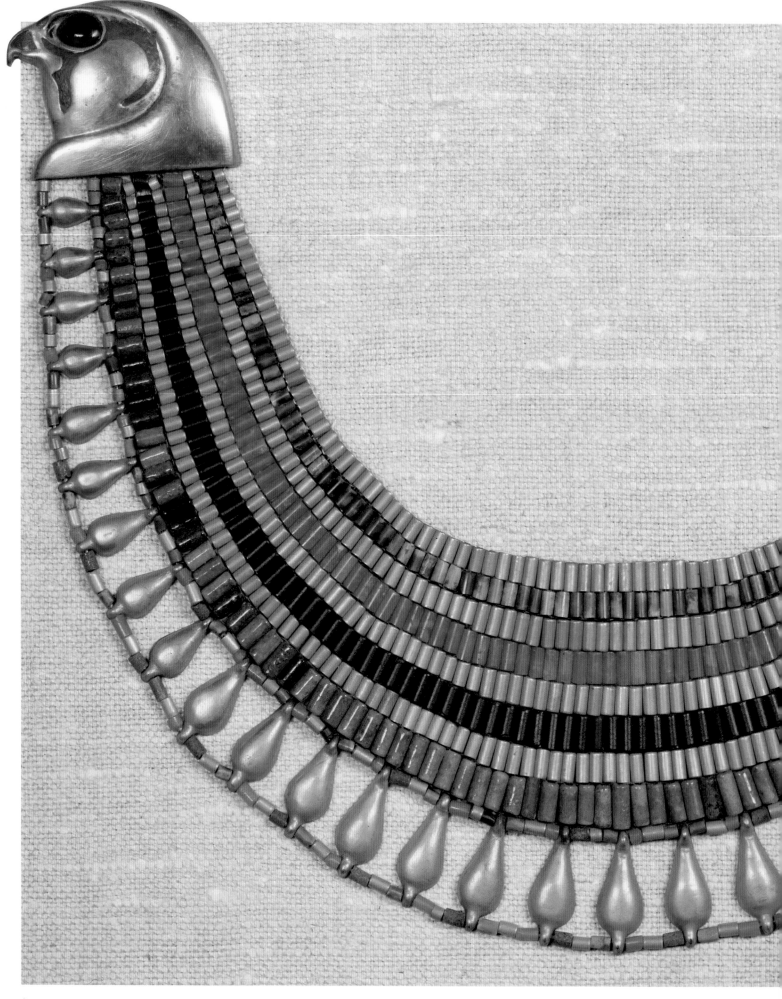

Wall Painting. Two craftsmen are shown at work in this copy of a painting found on the wall of an Egyptian tomb. The man to the right is using bow drills to bore holes in the beads that are going to be strung by his partner. Between them is a finished broad collar and a basket with unstrung beads or thread. Bow drills had been in use for thousands of years before the fifteenth century B.C., when the artist depicted these men busy at work. The technique is so practical it is still used today. The cutting power of the drill is increased by adding sand or emory as an abrasive. Larger beads are drilled from each end with holes meeting in the middle. Although a craftsman would normally work with only one drill, this man is using three at once, a manifestation of great skill. The beads seem to have been embedded in plaster to hold them in place during the drilling process. Craftsmen such as these were formed into guilds by specialty, and artisans in various disciplines would work together under the supervision of an important bureaucratic functionary.

Falcon-Headed Collar. The Egyptian jeweler's art reached a peak during the Twelfth Dynasty (1850–1775 B.C.). This necklace was made near the end of that period. The terminals of the partly restored collar are exquisite representations of the falcon-headed Horus. The broad collar with simple end pieces, called a *wesekh,* had been in use since at least the Fourth Dynasty (2613–1494 B.C.). It quickly became a common item in the costume of the Egyptian aristocracy. The falcon-headed version, however, is predominantly a funerary item, and this necklace was made as such for a woman named Senebtisi. Her tomb had been desecrated by robbers in antiquity, but they had not opened her coffin. In 1907 an expedition of The Metropolitan Museum of Art found the tomb. This necklace was imbedded in the linen wrapping her body. The terminals were originally made by burnishing gold foil over a mold and the resulting form was then filled with plaster. The large gold beads were constructed in the same manner. The eyes of Horus are carnelian, accentuated with an outline of blue pigment. The smaller beads are of gold, turquoise, carnelian, and faience. It has been possible to restore this necklace to its original beauty because of the careful recording that was made of the arrangement of the beads during the excavation.

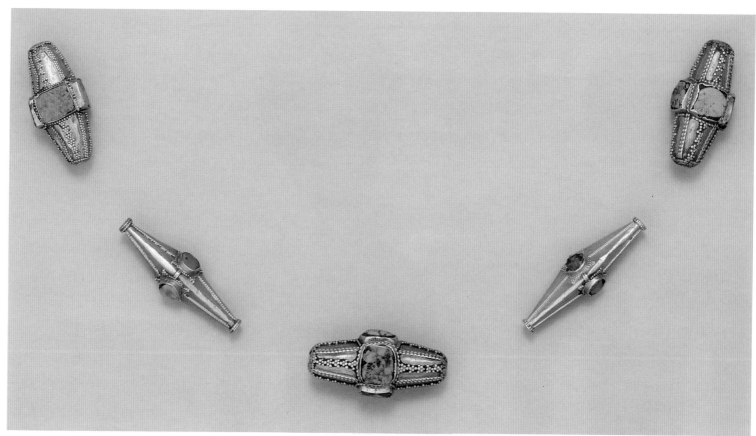

Beads from a Necklace. Beads were probably the earliest type of personal adornment. Shells, bones, and teeth worked into beads that are at least 20,000 to 30,000 years old have been found at several sites. Since then virtually every culture has developed different methods of elaborating on the bead form. Some beads were thought to be invested with talismanic powers, but most beads, like these examples, have been worn simply because they enhance the appearance of the person wearing them. These extraordinary gold beads, fabricated in Saudi Arabia during the nineteenth or early twentieth century, are an example of the beautifully complex works of art that can appear in bead form. Set with large turquoises, the hollow beads are embellished with fine gold granulation and swagged wire that simulates lines of granulation. These beads were originally strung on a necklace that probably included sections of irregularly shaped turquoise and coral beads. The complete piece would have been a marvel of richness and color.

Spherical and Biconical Beads. Spanning more than a millennium, the history of Islamic jewelry is both long and illustrious. The goldwork of the Fatimid era during the eleventh and twelfth centuries is the most accomplished and decoratively complex period within this history. These two beads, made during the eleventh century, appear to be two of only five such beads known. The light, airy construction of open filigree is covered with tiny grains of granulation. The beautifully executed scrolls and the delicacy of these beads belie the extraordinary technical difficulties that had to be surmounted to create them.

The Arab Jeweler. Charles Sprague Pearce lived in Boston until 1872, when he went to Paris to pursue a career as a painter. During the winter of 1873/74, he spent four months traveling and sketching along the Nile with a fellow art student. That trip probably provided the inspiration for this painting, which was first exhibited at the Paris Salon in 1882. The nearly life-size figure is surrounded by the accoutrements of his trade: anvil and tools rest by his feet, and partially worked materials, like the coral and lapis lazuli beads that have been threaded on gold shafts, lie at his side. The absorbed focus of the jeweler is centered on a bed of coals where sparks fly. Using his cheeks like a bellows, he blows a constant and concentrated stream of air into the center of the fire. This technique creates a spot of intensified heat, which he uses to melt a tiny piece of solder, binding the gold ornament he holds in the tongs to the strip of gold lying across the coals. The sitter is a powerful embodiment of the creative energy of all jewelers who have produced such beauty through the centuries.

Tabwa Figures. The Tabwa people live in southeastern Zaire and northeastern Zambia, in the area bordered by lakes Tanganyika and Mweru. About 1860 their arts began to flourish as a result of the Tabwa chiefs' sudden increase in power and wealth garnered from the slave and ivory trade. These sculptures portray the traditional modes of Tabwa body decoration. They wear strings of tiny glass beads that were among the European luxury goods exported to Africa for over a thousand years. They also have elaborate hair styles, but their significant decoration is the symmetrical pattern of raised cicatrices (scars) arranged in parallel lines on the forehead, cheeks, torso, and back. These patterns were intended to be both erotic and symbolic. For the Tabwa scarification was a means of perfecting the body through motifs alluding to positive social values and cosmological principles.

Three Necklaces. The Franks were a Germanic tribe who began to expand their territory in the third century, reaching the height of their power under Charlemagne in the eighth. During this period of the Great Migrations (fourth–seventh centuries), despite war, conquest, and the displacement of vast numbers of people from Mongolia to the tip of Spain, the manufacture and trade in beads continued. The beads in these necklaces were found in a Frankish burial ground and date from the fourth to the seventh centuries. Each necklace contains a variety of glass, paste, and stone beads. Glass was made as early as the second millennium B.C., and its first use was probably in decorative beads. By the time of the Roman hegemony, there were glass-bead manufactories throughout the Empire. The Franks maintained the glass works established by the Romans and eventually developed their own distinctive bead style, but the green melon-shaped beads on these necklaces are probably Roman. An unusual item in this collection is on the necklace at the top left, a bead from Syria or Egypt depicting a face.

Salome with the Head of Saint John the Baptist. After watching his stepdaughter's famous dance of the veils, Herod promises to grant whatever she wishes. Obeying her mother, Salome demands the head of John the Baptist. Andrea Solario (Italian, ca. 1460–1524) has depicted the grisly moment when "his head was brought in a charger, and given to the damsel" (Matthew 14:11). The artist has dressed and adorned Salome in the sumptuous manner of the early sixteenth century. Attached to the front of her fabric diadem is a gold jewel set with a table-cut ruby and four pearls. At her forehead is a *ferronière* with a gold-set aquamarine, a pale blue-green gem that derives its name from the Latin for "water of the sea." Salome's necklace has been strung with urn-shaped beads, probably of jet, and pearls whose luster matches that of her pale skin. Solario has carefully placed the pendant so that the bow holding the top of Salome's chemise is partially hidden by it. The loops of the bow are visible beneath the large pearl, and the ends of the bow peek out from the corners of the sapphire setting. In this way the gold string has been visually incorporated into the sapphire pendant. Her garment has been studded with pearls, rubies, and sapphires. Both the ruby and the sapphire were popular among the aristocracy by the time of the Renaissance. No stone, however, was as costly as the ruby. According to Benvenuto Cellini, a ruby's value in 1560 was eight times that of a diamond. Even today a ruby is generally the most precious of gems.

Necklace. This lavish necklace, made in Northern India in the eighteenth or nineteenth century, would have been worn with many other jewels, as in the earlier wall hanging to the right. Fabricated from gold, the necklace is set with cabochon diamonds and rubies. The stones that appear to be emeralds are actually rock crystal set in place over green foil. This deceptive technique has been used by jewelers since the earliest civilizations. The small pearls strung around the links and the pendants embellish the petal-like motif.

Wall Hanging. The inspiration that flowers give to Indian design is fully evident in this detail from a large textile wall hanging. Seen strolling through the lush garden of a princely palace in the 1640s, three ladies wear a profusion of jewelry that might well have been plucked from the garden itself. Depicted here are pearls, precious stones, and gold fashioned to look like floral garlands around their necks and bouquets of blossoms in their hair. Unfortunately, the gold and the gems of such magnificent pieces of jewelry were so precious that most have been broken up and do not survive in their original form.

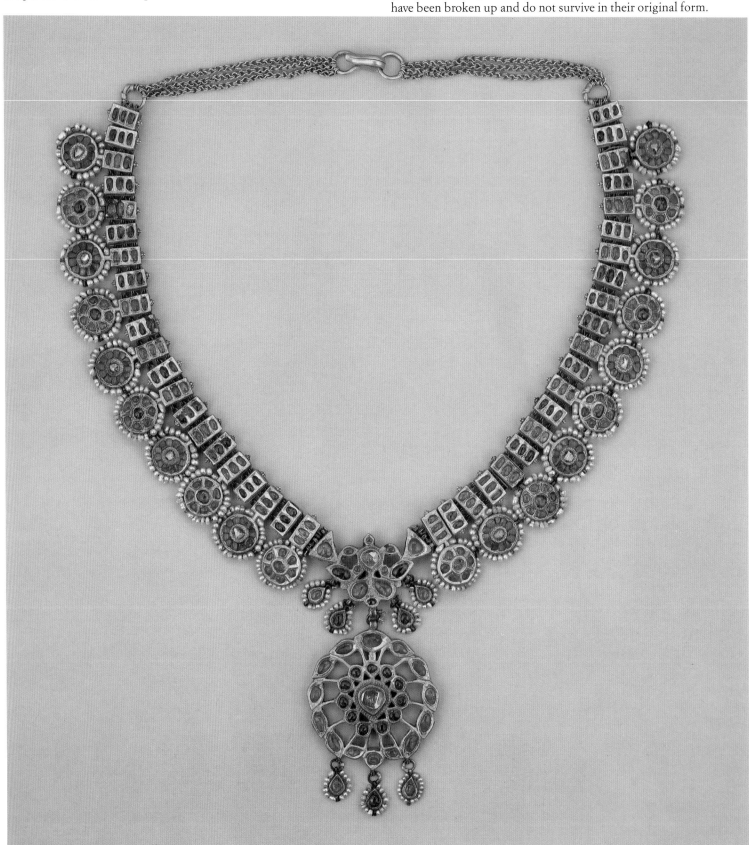

Maria Maddalena Baroncelli, Wife of Tommaso Portinari. A member of the large Florentine community in Bruges, the middle-aged Tommaso Portinari was partner and manager of the Bruges branch of the Medici bank when he married fourteen-year-old Maria Baroncelli. A handsome and highly ambitious man, he was already a prominent patron of the arts at the time of the marriage in 1470. About a year later he commissioned Hans Memling (Flemish, act. about 1465–d. 1494) to paint a half-length devotional triptych. This portrait of Maria is the right panel. Her simple black dress trimmed with white fur and her plain hat, a henin, provide a stark backdrop for her exquisite necklace. Tendrils of gold weave a frame around three types of enameled openwork rosettes. The red flower is centered with a sapphire, the white with a ruby, and the gray-blue with a pearl. Round jet or onyx beads dot the top of the necklace, and small teardrops of gold and bluish-gray enameled wire dangle from the base. Her only other jewelry is a simple wedding band set with a ruby and a sapphire. The necklace was clearly a prized possession, because about seven years later Maria wore it again in an altarpiece painted by Hugo van der Goes. In that portrait her henin is extravagantly decorated with pearls in the form of T's and M's. We know from X-ray examination that Memling originally included this pearl embellishment in his painting as well, but his deliberate simplification of the henin creates a far more dramatic setting for this unique necklace.

Saint Barbara. This lindenwood statue was made in Alsace around 1500. Legend has it that in the third century Saint Barbara, who had converted to Christianity, was beheaded by her pagan father. Martyred in Nicodemia, near Constantinople, she became a popular saint throughout the Christian world. In this representation she wears a necklace similar in design to Maria Portinari's but much simpler, with intertwined bows and pendants of oak leaves.

The Ch'ien-lung Emperor as a Young Man. The necklace worn by the eighteenth-century emperor in this painting on silk from the nineteenth century is the Manchu version of Tibetan Buddhist prayer beads. Called "Mandarin chains" by foreigners, they were worn by the royal family and members of the court. Sumptuary laws prescribed who could wear which types of beads, from the rare and costly coral and jade that the emperor wears here to the glass beads worn by low-ranked noblemen. The necklace follows a specific formula by which four groups of twenty-seven beads are separated by four large beads called "Buddha heads." The auxiliary strings, one on his right and two on his left, are made up of two groups of five amber beads each. Mandarin officials used these necklaces like abacuses, with each of the thirty beads serving as a counter. The large Buddha-head beads in this painting are made of jade. Jade has been used as a gemstone in China for over 7,000 years, and the art of jade carving reached one of its finest periods during the early reign of Ch'ien Lung. There are two kinds of jade. Originally, the Chinese used only nephrite from eastern China and central Asia, but over the past 150 years they have also worked imported jadeite from Burma.

Portrait of a Lady. This lovely young woman may be the daughter of Francesco Sassetti, a business adviser to the Medicis and a benefactor of the painter Domenico Ghirlandaio (Florentine, ca. 1448–94). The artist, who headed one of the best-organized and busiest workshops in Florence, painted this portrait about 1490. The necklace of large coral beads holds a gold pendant enhanced with two enameled florets and three pendant pearls. Ghirlandaio began his training in his father's goldsmith workshop, which may account for the exacting detail with which he has rendered this impressive necklace.

Virgin and Child. Jewels have not always been worn solely as beautiful adornments. Through the ages many gems and other materials have been invested with amuletic powers. In many cultures coral has been regarded as especially efficacious. According to Albertus Magnus, a German scholar of the thirteenth century, clear scientific proof existed that coral could staunch the flow of blood from a wound, cure madness, and give its owner wisdom. The Chinese believed that, in combination with other stones, coral could actually prolong the wearer's life. An eleventh-century Arab physician thought it promoted good humor. The most pervasive and persistent belief about coral, however, which began in pagan Rome and persisted after the advent of Christianity, was that wearing coral was the surest way to protect children from harm. In this painting by Joos van Cleve (Flemish, act. 1507–40/1) the Christ Child wears a necklace of coral beads. The branch-shaped pendant, however, is what provides the protection, for people believed that to exert its magical power, the coral must not have been worked.

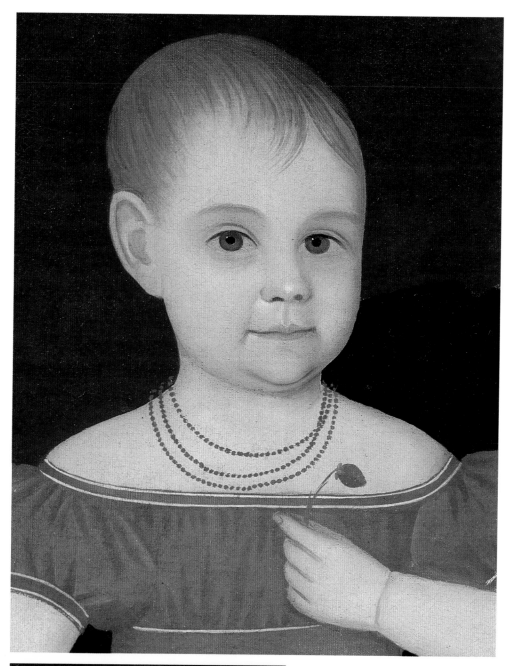

Mrs. Mayer and Daughter. Ammi Phillips (American, 1788–1865) was one of the most prolific and talented folk artists of the nineteenth century. In this painting from the early 1830s, the daughter wears a delicate three-strand necklace of coral beads. Although few people in the nineteenth century believed in the amuletic value of coral to protect children, it remained a favorite christening gift. Girls were given necklaces like the one in this painting, while boys received rattles with coral stems that could be sucked to aid in teething. Coral is actually the remains of living organisms—the exoskeletons of colonies of tiny sea animals, found mostly in the Mediterranean and Red seas. Traded over great distances since Paleolithic times, coral continues to be a popular component of jewelry.

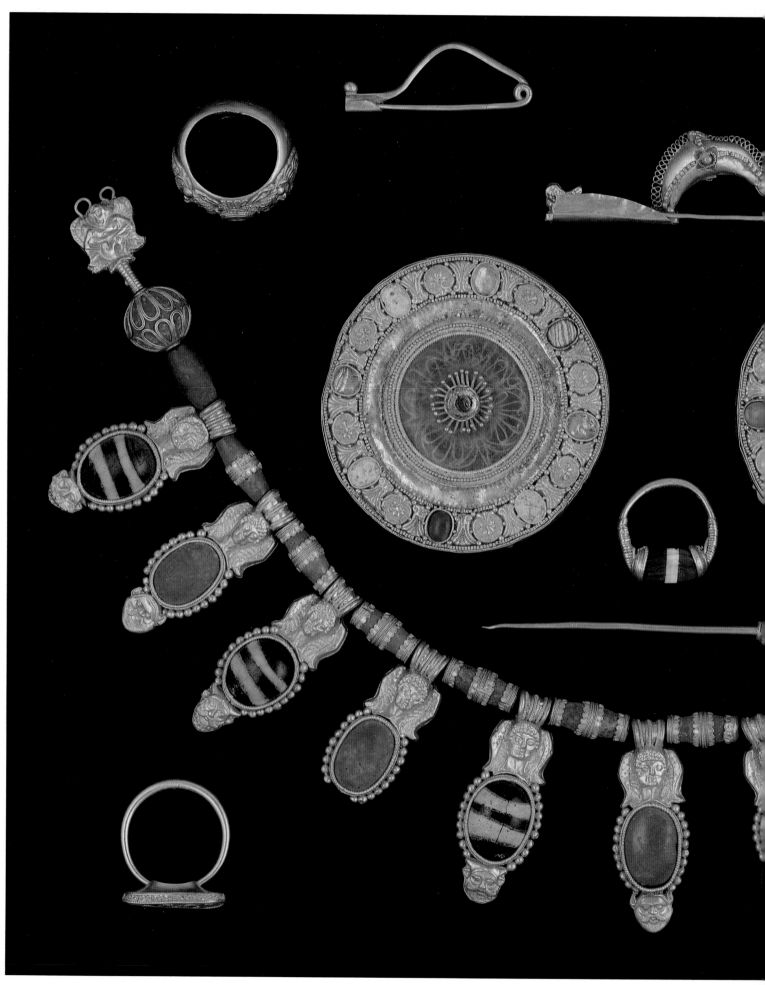

Etruscan Jewelry. The contents of their tombs reveal the considerable wealth of the Etruscans and demonstrate their predilection for elegant and costly jewelry. The burial chamber of an Etruscan woman, opened more than 150 years ago, yielded this opulent parure. The necklace has a strikingly rhythmic design with alternating solid and striated agates. The most ornate of the three fibulae has a leech-shaped bow with filigree decoration. The fibulae and the stickpin were not primarily decorative; their main function was to secure clothing. The centers of the two large disk earrings are made of rock crystal that has been backed with filigree wires. The outer bands have been set with carnelian and agate, both common materials in Etruscan jewelry. The origin of the Etruscans is a mystery, but there is evidence that they were established in the area now known as Tuscany by 900 B.C. During the fifth century B.C., at the height of their power, they controlled much of northern Italy and through trade had contact with other civilizations around the Mediterranean. From the beginning the Etruscans were superlative metalworkers, both in bronze and in precious metals. Through their contacts with the Greek colonies to the south, the range of techniques, forms, and iconography at their disposal was significantly enlarged.

Engraving of a Pendant. After the mid-sixteenth century, a revolution occurred in the process of jewelry design: jewelers began to publish their designs in sets of engravings. One of the most influential of these jewelers was Hans Collaert. In 1573 Collaert's son produced engravings based on his father's designs and published them in Antwerp. This enchanting pendant is from a set of prints published in 1582. When finished, the jewel would have been similar to the pendant illustrated at the right. Since engravings were used as diagrams for copying jewelry, they did not include the most exotic element of many Renaissance pendants: the baroque pearl. These unique, irregularly shaped pearls were often incorporated as the torsos of mythological creatures or the tails of dragons.

Venus and Cupid on a Marine Monster. This exquisite pendant was made in either Germany or Italy at the end of the sixteenth century.

We cannot be sure exactly where many Renaissance jewels were made because of the widespread use of engravings. These publications were distributed throughout Europe, and jewelers freely copied the designs. Here the body of the monster and the two riders are enameled; rubies and diamonds set in pyramidal collets add glittering accents. Pendants of this type were not only suspended from necklaces but were also worn on sleeves and hats.

Christ Blessing. In this detail of a painting by Ludger tom Ring the Younger (German, 1522–84), the eighteen-year-old daughter of the donor wears a large pendant typical of the Renaissance but more restrained than those above. (See page 82.)

Portrait of a Young Princess. The painter of this beautifully composed panel has been called the Master of Moulins and is now thought to be Jean Hey (French, act. about 1480–1500). The subject is probably the daughter of the Austrian Emperor Maximilian I, portrayed at the age of ten or eleven in 1490–91, when she was betrothed to Charles VIII, king of France. She is wearing a rather large pendant for a little girl, one more befitting her station than her size. A grand ruby and another cabochon gem are set in an enameled fleur-de-lis and finished with a pendant pearl. This was a time of great unhappiness for Margaret, for she was lodged in a foreign household and unhappily betrothed. As she clutches her rosary made of large pearls with a gold paternoster bead, she seems to be praying for the deliverance that finally came when the betrothal was dissolved in 1491.

ABOVE LEFT **Egyptian Crescent-shaped Pendant.** The art of Egypt during the reign of the Fatimids (A.D. 969–1171) is noteworthy for a surprising increase in the use of human and animal motifs. This period is also marked by a high level of craftsmanship. The goldwork is especially fine with elaborate designs like those on this pendant, which is constructed in filigree on a gold grid. The use of crescent-shaped ornaments was borrowed from Byzantine art, as was the technique of cloisonné enamel, employed here for the birds in the center. This pendant would have been framed by strands of pearls or beads of precious or semi-precious stones, laced through the gold hoops around the edge.

ABOVE RIGHT **French Pendant.** This pendant of gold and enamel, one of a series depicting the four seasons, was made by René Lalique (French, 1860–1945) at the turn of the twentieth century. The sycamore leaves and golden fruit cascading from the woman's hair evoke autumn. Lalique was a leading figure in the Art Nouveau movement, which began in the 1880s and lasted into the first decades of the twentieth century. Undulating forms and expressive new uses of translucent enamel were hallmarks of Art Nouveau jewelry.

MIDDLE LEFT **South American Pendant.** This pendant, which is 5¾ inches high, was made between the seventh and twelfth centuries in the high plateau area of the Andes that is situated in southern Colombia and extends into Ecuador. The art of this plateau is distinctive and markedly uniform. In this piece anthropormorphic and zoomorphic references have been completely abstracted, resulting in a bold ornament of pure line. It is a design of universal appeal, resembling both ancient calligraphy and modern sculpture.

BELOW LEFT AND RIGHT **French Pendant.** The *commesso* is a rare form of jewelry in which semiprecious stones are carved in the shape of a figure or a head and combined with gold, and sometimes enamel, to form a unified design. The technique flourished briefly in the rarefied atmosphere of the sixteenth-century French court, where this pendant was made between 1550 and 1555. The front of the pendant shows the chalcedony figure of Prudence sitting in front of a brilliant blue enameled background and peering into a diamond mirror as she grasps a serpent. The reverse is an enameled scene of the goddess Diana and her hounds based on a design by Charles Etienne Delaune (French, ca. 1518–83), the principal medalist to Henry II. This pendant was listed in the king's inventory, and it is interesting to note that Prudence was associated with Henry's wife, Catherine de'Medici, and Diana with his mistress, Diane de Poîtiers.

Federico Gonzaga. Though not in miniature form, this poignant painting was created as a way of preserving the image of a beloved child. Isabella d'Este commissioned this portrait of her ten-year-old son in 1510 just before he was sent to the papal court to be held as a hostage for his father. Finishing the portrait in less than a week, Francesco Francia (Bolognese, act. by 1482–d. 1517/18) included a lovely gold-link collar. Collars were worn by men during the sixteenth century, often as a heraldic accoutrement, but the delicacy of this necklace seems scaled for a child and was perhaps made especially for Federico Gonzaga. Initially trained as a goldsmith, the artist signed his letter thanking Isabella d'Este for payment "Francia, Goldsmith at Bologna."

A Mother's Pearls (Portraits of the Artist's Children). The art and sentiment of the miniature was brought to the American colonies from Europe, where they were presentation pieces given by sovereigns in recognition of service and exchanged privately as the most intimate of mementos. American miniatures were also given and received as tokens of affection. Thomas Seir Cummings (American, 1804–94) painted these nine miniature portraits of his children around 1841. Each watercolor on ivory was painted in exact and minute detail and mounted in a necklace of gold as a gift to the artist's wife.

William Roper and Margaret More Roper. Hans Holbein the Younger (German, 1497/98–1543) went to England in 1526 where, through their mutual friend Erasmus, he met and lived with Sir Thomas More and his family for eighteen months. It was there that he probably first met Henry VIII, who later employed him. Holbein had already achieved an international reputation as a portrait painter, but in his capacity as goldsmith's designer to the king, he produced some of the finest jewelry designs of the age as well. These two paintings on vellum set in pendant frames were made in 1538 when William was 42 and Margaret was 30, three years after the king had her father, Sir Thomas, executed. She was a learned and devoted daughter, and her husband eventually wrote a biography of his father-in-law, one of the first biographies written in the English language.

Portrait of a Woman. Cameo carving began to proliferate in Greece following the reign of Alexander the Great late in the fourth century B.C. The sardonyx, which was the favorite stone of the ancient cameo engravers, came from India. Newly expanded trade with that area after Alexander's conquests in the East greatly enhanced the development of the art. Although ancient cameos were highly valued during medieval times, the craft of cameo carving was rarely practiced. A new interest in cameos flourished during the Renaissance. While ancient cameos continued to be cherished, the art of cameo carving was revived, and both old and new stones were placed in magnificent settings. This portrait was painted in the style of Hans Holbein during the second half of the sixteenth century. The cameo in the lady's brooch has heads adorned in the ancient style, but we do not know whether this is an ancient or contemporary stone, since the subjects of Renaissance cameos ranged from the deities of ancient myth to portraits of contemporary sovereigns. The pendant, which hangs from a chain of black-enameled gold links, appears to be an adaptation of a design by Holbein.

Pendant with a Head of Jupiter. This pendant exemplifies two revivals that occurred in the nineteenth century and shows the meticulous workmanship of that period. The Neoclassical revival, which had begun in the late eighteenth century, continued to flourish in the nineteenth and created renewed interest in cameos. This cameo was probably made in Italy during the early nineteenth century. Although the main portion is carved from traditional agate, the broken bottom portion has been repaired with ivory or horn. The frame is styled like a Renaissance setting, but it too is a copy made in the latter part of the nineteenth century.

Cameo Portrait of the Emperor Augustus. This masterpiece of sardonyx may date from the reign of Claudius (A.D. 41–54). During this period the cameo engraver's art reached a high level of excellence, and here Augustus is rendered in the flat, low relief perfected by the ancient carvers. Augustus, who founded the Roman empire and reigned from 27 B.C. to A.D. 4, is depicted as a god, wearing an aegis, the scaly cape of Athena with trailing snakes.

OPPOSITE **Anna Watson Stuart.** In this portrait by Daniel Huntington (American, 1816–1906), completed in the 1860s, the sitter is wearing a bracelet of six cameo links, each surrounded by seed pearls. The cameos are portraits of Mrs. Stuart and her husband, as well as their four children. They were carved by the renowned American sculptor Augustus Saint Gaudens between 1861 and 1867. Although large shell cameos were fashionable during this time, those in the bracelet are made of the far more precious onyx.

Cameo Set. This parure is a beautiful example of a nineteenth-century genre called "archaeological jewelry." The magnificent ancient treasure discovered at several sites early in the century fueled the desire of women to be adorned in the elegant style of the classical era. The two premier stone carvers of the time were a father and son, Tommaso and Luigi Saulini. After studying in Rome under the famous Danish sculptor Bertel Thorvaldsen, Tommaso established himself as a stone carver around 1836, and an active family business was carried on until Luigi's death in 1883. It was Luigi who carved the cameos in this suite, and the cameo in the tiara, entitled "The Toilet of Nausicaa," is considered his greatest work. The designs of both the cameo and the gold tiara were executed by Sir John Gibson (British, 1806–84), a renowned sculptor who worked in Rome for most of his life. Gibson obtained several important commissions for the Saulinis, whose work was esteemed throughout Europe. In fact, he served as intermediary in one of Luigi Saulini's more notable commissions, a double portrait cameo of Queen Victoria and Prince Albert. While evocative of ancient jewelry, the gold work in which the cameos are set is not as true to its archaeological antecedents as the work of another famous father-and-son team, Fortunato Pio and Alessandro Castellani. Key figures in the archaeological jewelry movement, the Castellanis strove to rediscover ancient techniques of working gold so that their jewelry would truly emulate classical models. In the process they created pieces of superb beauty. In the carving of stone and shell cameos, the work of the Saulinis in the mid-nineteenth century is likewise without peer.

Woman with a Parrot. The model for this masterful portrait by Edouard Manet (French, 1832–83) is Victorine Meurent, who also posed for Manet's celebrated *Luncheon on the Grass.* Here, attired in a silk pink dressing gown, she wears around her throat one of the ubiquitous jewels of the nineteenth century, the locket. Lockets held mementos, the locks of a loved one's hair, miniature portraits, or photographs. Although they were quite ornate at the beginning of the century, by the 1860s, when this portrait was painted, the cases had become much plainer. This locket is suspended from a black ribbon, and a man's monocle hangs from a thin chain.

Locket. The back of this wonderful locket, which was made in France between 1620 and 1640, was decorated by using the champlevé enamel technique. The pattern is a rare example of the ornamentation called "peapod," a stylized representation of botanical forms. In the early seventeenth century there was a great interest in flowers all over Europe, and this naturally led to floral representation in jewelry. The style was popularized by French engravers, and there is an engraving of a pattern very similar to the one on this locket by Gédéon l'Egaré (French, 1615–76). The cover is a polished rock crystal set in an enameled gold bezel, which is hinged to the back of the case. The locket, which is 1½ inches high, may originally have held a miniature portrait.

Bulla. A hollow container with a stopper, the bulla was first made by the Etruscans and later adopted by the Romans. It was worn as a pendant around the arm or the neck, sometimes with several together on one chain, and might contain a charm or perfume. Children also wore bullae: gold for the offspring of noble families and leather for freedmen's families. This gold Etruscan bulla of about the third century B.C. has a stamped design showing a man between two genii.

Statue of a Young Woman. In her elaborate clothing and jewelry, this statue represents a woman from fourth- or third-century B.C. Lavinium, a site just south of Rome. The elaborate pendants and the arm bracelet appear to be reproduced from molds of actual jewelry, some decorated with classical themes. The lower necklace has been strung with bullae of various shapes. The bulla was worn on a flexible chain or string so that the stopper could be opened without removing the bulla, enabling the wearer to sniff the scent inside.

Portrait of the Princesse de Broglie. The princess was a great beauty and a highly respected woman, the embodiment of the best of the Second Empire aristocracy. Ingres (French, 1780–1867) completed this painting in 1853 when the princess was twenty-eight. Her earrings are shimmering cascades of seed pearls. On her right wrist she wears a bracelet of red-enameled and diamond-set gold links, and on her left she has wrapped a rope of pearls. But what attracts our attention above all is the handsome gold pendant on a fine double loop-in-loop chain. In the year this portrait was painted, the wearing of classically styled jewelry was the latest fashion, and both antique jewelry and contemporary reproductions were readily available. What graces the neck of the princess, however, is no imitation but a genuine Roman bulla.

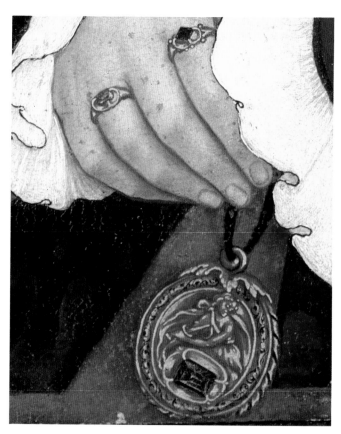

Pendant. This extraordinarily rare sixteenth-century Italian jewel has been carved entirely from a substance assumed to be ambergris, which has been decorated with gold, enamel, and precious stones. Ambergris is a soft secretion of the sperm whale, which on exposure to the air gradually hardens and develops a sweet odor. This pendant then was a delight to the nose as well as to the eye. It depicts a woman and three children, accompanied by two musicians and three smaller enamel figures carrying flowers. Like other ornate Renaissance pendants, this could have been worn suspended from a necklace or fastened to the sleeve.

Lady Lee (Margaret Wyatt). This noble portrait of a thirty-four-year-old woman is a sixteenth-century copy after Hans Holbein. Her black-and-white French hood is trimmed with pearls over the crown and at the ears. She has looped a gold chain around her neck and placed two gem-set rings on her fingers. Her sleeves flash with glittering aglets. These dress ornaments were generally designed in suites. Constructed so that they could be attached to a garment or a hat, aglets decorated the large skirts and sleeves that were the Elizabethan fashion. Pieces of ambergris were occasionally placed inside the ornaments so that they would exude a sweet smell. The gold pomander hanging from Lady Lee's girdle provides another method of perfuming the air. Given the level of hygiene in the sixteenth century, it isn't surprising that many forms of scented jewelry were created.

ETATIS · · SVÆ · 34 ·

41

Portrait of a Young Man. Painted by Bronzino (Italian, 1503–72) in the late 1530s when he was at the peak of his powers, this is a portrait of an aristocratic Florentine. A perfect complement to the young man's insouciant pose is his rakish hat covered with aglets. A popular fashion in Germany and England as well as Italy, aglets ornamented hats worn by Henry VIII in a number of his portraits. Some appliqués in the Renaissance were made of plain gold, while others were enameled or set with jewels. They were also made in representational forms, such as flowers, frogs, and fruit. The practice of enhancing men's clothing with ornaments was not a new one. The Etruscans, Greeks, and Romans followed the practice. Even in the fifth century B.C. the Scythians used magnificent miniature animals to adorn the garments of their warriors.

Portrait of a Noblewoman. Painted by an unknown British artist in the late sixteenth century, this sitter has not been identified, but she has been portrayed as the quintessential Elizabethan lady. With more than ninety enameled gold and gem-set broochlike aglets visible on her dress, she has combined several suites to stunning effect. (Mary, Queen of Scots owned one of the largest single set of aglets, consisting of eighty-four pieces.) As if this ornamentation were not extravagant enough, the intersections of the fabric trellis on her bodice have been connected by rows of three pearls and topped by a huge aigrette worn as a brooch. In another portrait of the same woman, she wears this aigrette pinned at the shoulder of her puffed sleeve. As an added touch of elegance, her fan handle has been set with gems. Pearls are everywhere. Four rows of individually matched strands fit tightly around her neck, and two large pendant pearls dangle from her ears. Her transparent cloak has been trimmed with more pearls and ropes of them are wrapped around each wrist. It is possible that the sitter was a lady of the Elizabethan court and that some of these accoutrements were gifts from the Queen. Queen Elizabeth herself had a passion for pearls, as did several other queens of the time. One collection of pearls connected them all. At the time of the marriage of Mary, Queen of Scots to the French dauphin, his mother, Catherine de'Medici, gave Mary "six cordons of large pearls [and] about twenty-five separate from the others much larger and more beautiful." Catherine had these pearls with her when she first came to France to wed the man who would become King Henry II. After Mary's demise, Catherine attempted to retrieve the pearls but without success. Queen Elizabeth had bought them all for a fraction of their worth and declined to let them go.

The Empress Eugénie. The daughter of a Spanish grandee and his American wife, Eugénie de Montijo married Napoleon III, emperor of France, in 1853 when she was twenty-six. This charming portrait by Franz Xaver Winterhalter (German, 1805–73) was completed the next year. The empress was well known for her admiration of Marie Antoinette, and here she wears a contemporary adaptation of a late-eighteenth-century gown. Its trimmings of ribbon, lace, and ropes of pearls combine the styles of Louis XV and Louis XVI. Perhaps some of the pearls we see in this portrait are the same ones Consuelo Vanderbilt referred to when she wrote about her own marriage to the Duke of Marlborough: "My mother had given me all the pearls she had received from my father. There were two fine rows which had once belonged to Catherine of Russia and to the Empress Eugénie."

Portrait of a Woman with a Dog. Although painted by Jean Honoré Fragonard (French, 1732–1806) about 1769, this costume recalls that of the court of Maria de'Medici in the early seventeenth century and may indicate that the sitter is an actress. Except for an ornate brooch, pearls are her only jewelry. Pearls have been highly valued in many cultures over the centuries, and from earliest times have been seen as emblems of purity, beauty, and nobility. In China, records exist as far back as 2200 B.C. of freshwater pearls being given as precious gifts. Persian noblemen wore a single pearl earring in the right ear, a practice adopted later by the Greeks. Pearls were so valuable in Rome that Suetonius reported General Vitellius paid the expenses of a military campaign by selling a single pearl earring belonging to his mother.

Saint Justina of Padua. An Early Christian martyr of noble birth, Saint Justina is traditionally depicted in an elaborate costume. The coiffure and dress reflect the style of a wealthy Italian woman of the 1490s, when this picture was painted by Bartolomeo Montagna. Justina wears a lovely pearl necklace with a pearl-edged ruby pendant, and her head is splendidly adorned. A long piece of sheer blue fabric has been ingeniously knotted to secure the basic structure of her hairstyle. A dazzling jeweled net caps the back of her head and a hoop of gemstones, pearls, and gold restrains the fall of her long, luxuriant hair. She serenely holds a palm frond, which is one of the symbols of her martyrdom. The other symbol is more grisly, but has been quite discreetly portrayed here: the dagger piercing her heart.

Portrait of a Young Woman. Piero del Pollaiuolo and his brother Antonio collaborated in a highly successful workshop in fifteenth-century Florence. Although Antonio was trained as a goldsmith, it is Piero who lovingly renders the jewels in this portrait. The sitter's hair has been plaited with pearls and set with several delightful ornaments. A touch of coral forms the center of the jeweled flowers, whose petals have been enameled a deep blue. They are surrounded by pearls and tiny gold pendants, which would have shimmered as she moved. A more elaborate piece, set with a ruby, crowns her coiffure.

The Wife of Abraham Benchimol and One of Their Daughters. Eugène Delacroix (French, 1798–1863) painted this sumptuous watercolor in 1832, when he accompanied the Count de Mornay to Morocco on his mission as goodwill ambassador to the sultan, Abd-ar-Rahman. Abraham Benchimol was the Jewish interpreter for the French delegation, and in depicting his family, Delacroix presents a faithful picture of their costume. Although the mother displays no jewelry, the daughter is wearing a gold necklace and two strands of coral beads. Her elaborate jeweled head ornaments are almost identical to the actual examples pictured below.

Pair of Gold Head Ornaments. These pieces were created in Morocco in the eighteenth or nineteenth century. They are fabricated of chased gold sheet and wire and set with rubies, emeralds, topazes, pearls, and glass. As we can see in Delacroix's painting, the triangular ornaments are worn hooked to a headdress near the top of the head. The circular ornaments are suspended from chains attached to the upper jewels. The jewel-encrusted portions face forward, giving the same appearance as earrings.

Matilda Stoughton de Jaudenes. The sitter was an American, who at sixteen married Josef de Jaudenes, whose father served as Spanish consul in Boston for thirty years. Although her opulent, fashionable costume and the display of richly jeweled ornaments would have been regarded as excessive and in bad taste for a young American, this splendor, like the fan she holds, was completely appropriate for the wife of a wealthy and ambitious Spanish diplomat. A contemporary diarist acidly compared the couple to little dolls. This 1794 portrait by Gilbert Stuart (American, 1755–1828) is a superb example of the brilliant style he employed just after his return to the United States from England.

Pendants and Earrings. These opulent Spanish and Portuguese jewels were made in the eighteenth and nineteenth centuries. All are made of gold, and the two middle pendants are set with diamonds. The earrings at the left are set with emeralds, those at the right with jacinths. Jewelers in Portugal and Spain accommodated the desire of fashionable women for versatility by designing jewels that contained linked components. The tiered earrings could be worn at several different lengths simply by removing or adding the appropriate number of elements. The gem-set bow, or *lazo,* could be worn alone or with its additional pendants. Brooches in the shape of bows, called *sévignés* in France, originated in the seventeenth century and were a favorite motif in Europe for several centuries.

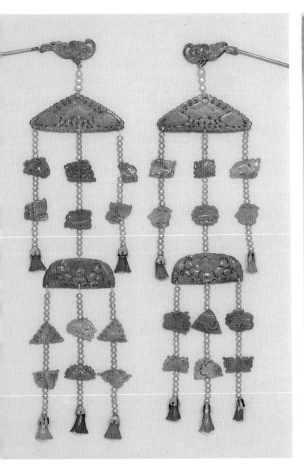

Hairpins. These eighteenth-century hairpins were probably part of a theatrical headdress. They have been strung with carved amber and pearls. The heads of the pins are in the shape of bats, a common Chinese decorative motif symbolizing happiness and longevity. The bats and the terminals of the danglers have been decorated with kingfisher feathers, imported from southeast Asia and greatly valued as a material of embellishment in China. The feathers are cut and appliquéd onto the metal base, giving an appearance akin to iridescent enamel.

Empress of the Yung-cheng Emperor (r. 1723–35). This nineteenth-century painting on silk was made by an unknown artist. Like the emperor on page 20, the empress wears a "Mandarin chain" necklace, but hers incorporates four large crystal beads instead of the emperor's jade. Both of her ears have been pierced three times so that she can wear six earrings, each hung with two pearls. Her headpiece has been adorned with clouds and flowers of enameled gold. The pendant portions of a set of hairpins dangle behind her ears. Ladies of the court began wearing these massive confections on their heads in the tenth century. They were more concerned about having a display of imaginative ornament than with the intrinsic value of the jewels contained in it. These elaborate headdresses remained in style until the early twentieth century, when revolution precipitated the downfall of the imperial family. Nowadays, a headdress is occasionally worn by brides.

Comb. Tiffany and Company was founded in New York in 1837 by Charles Lewis Tiffany and several partners. A businessman with a knack for predicting new trends, Tiffany made his company the premier American jeweler of the nineteenth century with the help of several key figures. Of prime importance was George Frederick Kunz, the firm's gem specialist from 1877 to 1932. By championing native American stones as well as buying extensively around the world, Kunz provided gems that enabled the company to create the sensational jewels that brought it renown. Another Tiffany success factor was a fortuitous change in the diamond market in the late nineteenth century. Production from the Indian diamond mines discovered in the seventeenth century began to decline in the eighteenth, and the Brazilian mines discovered in 1725 were also becoming less productive when, in 1866, diamonds were discovered in South Africa. The South African mines substantially increased the number of diamonds on the market, making them affordable for a far greater number of people than ever before. Made around 1910, this splendid comb is constructed from tortoiseshell and platinum and features a number of the beautiful diamonds for which the Tiffany firm was famous.

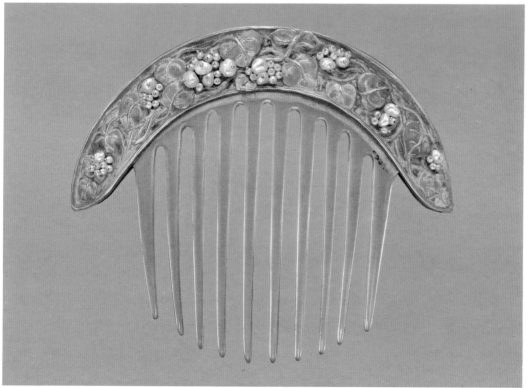

Comb. Although the Arts and Crafts Movement in America produced outstanding practitioners in furniture and pottery, only a few successful jewelers emerged. Among the best known of the Arts and Crafts jewelers was Florence Koehler (American, 1861–1944), who worked in Chicago. This exquisite comb, fabricated around 1905, has a crown of gold with enameled leaves on twisted vines and pearls bunched like grapes on a base of tortoiseshell or horn.

Chaplet of Gold Leaves. This delicate wreath of lapis lazuli and carnelian beads, with thin gold sheets hammered and chased in the form of beech leaves, was found encircling the head of a handmaiden who had been buried with her queen in a rich grave in the Royal Cemetery at Ur. Situated on the Euphrates River in southern Mesopotamia, Ur was one of the most important cities of the Sumerian culture. The site was excavated in the 1920s and 1930s by Sir Leonard Woolley. Along with this chaplet made between 2600 and 2500 B.C., the attendant wore two necklaces of gold and lapis lazuli, gold hair ribbons, and two silver hair rings. Since gold, silver, lapis, and carnelian are not found in Mesopotamia, the presence of these rich adornments attests to the wealth of the Early Dynastic Sumerians and to the existence of a complex system of trade that extended far beyond the Mesopotamian River valley.

Portrait of a Woman with a Fillet. This panel of the second century A.D. is from the Fayum, an Egyptian oasis where many Greeks settled during the Ptolemaic Period. The Greek settlers adopted some Egyptian customs, including mummification. Painted panels such as this served the function of the traditional mummy mask. The portraits on them, however, depicted current Mediterranean fashions, which accounts for the style of the jewelry. Fillets were worn from early Greek to late Roman times, being conferred by the state as a mark of honor or worn in religious processions. They were also used for funereal purposes, placed on the brow of the dead as a token of the person's victory in the battle of life. The type shown here was made of thin gold, cut and pressed to resemble leaves and and formed into wreaths with wires for stems.

Lady Playing the Kithara. The painted walls of a room, created between 40 and 30 B.C. in a villa at Boscoreale, about a mile from Pompeii, include large figures in various scenes against a red background. The murals are admired as excellent adaptations of Greek paintings, which reflect the erudition and worldliness of the villa's owner. The seated woman pictured here holds a kithara in her lap. Behind her stands a girl whose informal pose and resemblance to the older woman suggest that she is the kitharist's daughter. The pair may represent a Macedonian queen and princess; both wear similar gold diadems and gold hoop earrings. The style of the jewelry, like that of the painting, is Greek, for once the Romans took control of Greece, their assimilation of Greek art was immediate and direct.

TOP **Diadem.** This Greek diadem dates from the late fourth century B.C. The scene of Dionysos and Ariadne flanked by attendants playing musical instruments is depicted on the cut sheet of gold. The figures and decoration are executed in beautifully modulated low relief.

ABOVE **Herakles Knot.** This motif was often used as the centerpiece of a diadem. As in the painting, the diadem would have been worn on a high coiffure; the chains on the knot would have dangled on the forehead. Pliny wrote that the Herakles knot had the power to heal wounds.

Reliquary Bust of Saint Juliana. In 1376 the convent of Saint Juliana in Perugia was given the skull of their patron saint. This beguiling image of the young martyr once held that relic. The entire reliquary head up to the crown was hammered from a single sheet of copper. Hinges at the crown allowed the actual skull to be set inside.

Madonna and Child with Two Angels. This panel, painted about 1481 by Vittore Crivelli (Venetian, act. by 1465–d. 1501/2) is among his most beautiful works. The halos, crown, bandeaus, and brocaded borders of the Virgin's clothes are in gilt relief. The Christ Child and the two angels wear bandeaus of pearls with a gold-set cabochon gem. The central stone of the Virgin's brooch and those on two of the bandeaus may be rubies but they have the rich sherry color of a topaz. Although not a fashionable stone for secular jewelry during the Middle Ages, the topaz was used in ecclesiastical jewelry.

Queen Victoria. After the queen sat for him several times, Thomas Sully (American, 1783–1872) completed this oil sketch in May 1838, the month before her coronation. The jewels studied at the right are the emblems for the Order of the Garter, an order of knighthood founded in the fourteenth century. She wears the King George IV State Diadem, which was designed by her uncle in 1821 and then set with hired jewels. Using gems from the royal collection, the diadem was reset for Queen Victoria. The four diagonally pierced squares, called *crosses pattées,* and bouquets of the upper tier are pavé-set with diamonds, many of substantial size. The diamond base is framed by two circles of pearls. It is this diadem that Queen Elizabeth II is wearing in the portrait used for United Kingdom stamps. She has also had occasion to wear Victoria's diamond girandole earrings, a style inaugurated in the seventeenth century.

Venus and Cupid. Lorenzo Lotto was born and trained in Venice. In the mid-1520s he produced only two paintings with secular subjects, one of which was this work, in which Venus symbolically confers her blessing upon a bride and expresses her hope that the marriage will be long-lived and fruitful. The painting was inspired by classical marriage poems of a type known from the works of Catullus, Statius, and Claudian, and the symbolic elements are transformed by Lotto's genius into a masterpiece of the first rank, one of the most appealing of marriage paintings. The rose petals and the shell above the head of Venus are her attributes. The myrtle wreath was a feature of classical and Renaissance marriage ceremonies, and the small brazier is described in classical literature. The diadem, veil, and earrings, however, are like those worn by Venetian brides in the early sixteenth century. The diadem is set with pearls, sapphires, emeralds, rubies, and a diamond. The earring has a polished, uncut sapphire and a large pearl threaded on gold wire. The use of the sapphire as a gemstone dates back to the Etruscans. In the Middle Ages it was the preferred stone of both kings and bishops and was believed to be an antidote to poison. One of the most famous gems in history, the "Star of India," is a sapphire weighing over 563 carats.

Madame Paul Darras. The sitter met Renoir through mutual friends and commissioned this portrait in 1871. The artist here reveals his unfailing awareness of the feminine qualities of his subject. Light glints off her jewelry, which forms a striking contrast to her black fur-trimmed coat. The sitter's gold shield-shaped earrings are studded with dots of coral, and her large rectangular ring has been brushed with the purple of an amethyst. She wears a plain gold band and a pearl cluster ring on her left hand, and around her neck are a barely visible gold chain and locket. Although the display of jewelry is not particularly ostentatious, the portrait has been criticized as an "image of bourgeois opulence."

OPPOSITE, ABOVE LEFT **Greek Earrings.** This pair of earrings is one of the most beautiful ever found in the ancient world. They were made during the fourth century B.C. and form part of a set known as the "Ganymede jewelry," after the subject depicted on these earrings. The pendants of cast gold show the beautiful boy Ganymede being carried off by Zeus, who appears as an eagle. The illusion of their flight was conveyed when the earrings swayed.

OPPOSITE, ABOVE RIGHT **Byzantine Earrings.** Found on the island of Cyprus in 1902, these earrings of gold, pearls, and sapphires were probably made in Constantinople during the sixth or seventh century A.D. The free-swinging loop of pearls encompassing the sapphire pendant enhances the movement of the pieces. The Byzantine court held vast wealth, much of it displayed in jewelry. The Byzantines loved color and favored glittering precious stones and enamel in their personal jewelry.

MIDDLE LEFT **Langobardic Earrings.** In 568 the Longobards, a Germanic tribe, moved westward into northern Italy. There they ruled until their incorporation into the Frankish Kingdom by Charlemagne in 774. Their contact with the Byzantine Empire strongly influenced Langobardic jewelry design, especially in earrings. This alluring pair of gold basket earrings has been set with turquoise-colored glass beads, and tiny pearls have been wired to the centers.

MIDDLE RIGHT **Indian Earrings.** These sumptuous gold objects, called the Kronos earrings, were made during the first century B.C. Undoubtedly a royal commission, the fine craftsmanship with its exquisite granulation demonstrates that ancient Indian goldworking was on a level with any other major goldworking culture of that time. The size and weight of earrings such as these eventually would have distended the earlobe so that the ornaments rested on the wearer's shoulders.

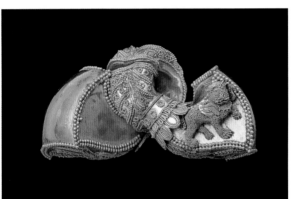

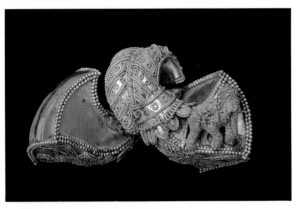

BELOW LEFT **Moroccan Earrings.** These fabulous seventeenth- to eighteenth-century earrings have several features that are reminiscent of Roman examples. The hoop ear wire hinged to the lower element is similar to the Byzantine earrings above, and the wrapped-wire method of suspending pearls and stones has remained basically unchanged since ancient times. The fronts have been set with emeralds and rubies, and the backs have been adorned by engraving and champlevé enamel.

BELOW RIGHT **Egyptian Earring.** While earrings had long been a favorite form of ornamentation elsewhere in the Near East, they were not widely worn in Egypt until about 1500 B.C. This stunning hoop from the late Eighteenth Dynasty (ca. 1400–1300 B.C.) is made of gold and inlaid with lapis lazuli. The pattern is probably intended to represent feathering.

Maya Whistle. The ancient Maya occupied a large area of southern Mexico and were a cultural entity distinct from their northern Mexican neighbors. While their history was a long one, the art for which they are best known was produced between A.D. 600 and 900. The imposing, paunchy figure in this Mayan ceramic work from the eighth century is clad in the full feathered attire associated with the magnificent bird costumes once worn by Maya warriors. On his chest, he wears a large disk that may be a mirror and in his ears are circular earflares. A tall headdress finishes the costume. The figure is actually a whistle. Ceramic figurines made either as whistles or rattles were deposited as burial offerings.

Earplug Frontal. Around A.D. 100 in what is now northern Peru, the Moche, also known as Mochica, began to emerge as the dominant political force. The enormous pyramid of adobe brick that they built in their capital was the largest man-made structure in ancient South America. The Moche were also master metalsmiths, creating beautiful objects in gold, silver, and copper. This earplug was made between 100 B.C. and A.D. 600. The spiderweb was cut from a sheet of gold and ornamented with dangling disks. The silver spider is attached to the center by its legs. The original inlay for the eyes and indentations in the body is now missing.

Vessel with Mythological Scene. His movement and vitality master-fully captured by the artist on this straight-sided ceramic Mayan vessel from the eighth century, the deity known as Chac-Xib-Chac engages in an energetic sacrificial dance. His elaborately wrapped hair waves above the enormous shells anchored in his ears. A great necklace with death's eyes and an upside-down vessel marked with the glyph for darkness from which a snake emerges, swings to the rhythm of the dance. The ankles and wrists of Chac-Xib-Chac are also adorned. The baby jaguar, whose paw and tail are visible on the right, will be sacrificed by the long-handled axe the deity wields in his right hand. The entire sacrificial tableau, including one of the Lords of Death, is depicted around the vessel. Although present interpretations of the specific meaning of this scene vary, it is generally read to imply a triumph over death itself.

Moche Ear Ornaments. Ear ornaments were popular personal adorn-ments throughout the ancient Americas, and in Peru those made of precious metal were quite large. During the Moche era a particularly impressive group of these ornaments with mosaic images on their wide frontals was created. The mosaics are composed of materials such as turquoise, chrysocolla, quartz, pyrite, and spondylus shell. In this pair, made in Peru between the third and sixth centuries, the mosaics have been set in gold. They depict winged, bird-headed (or masked) runners. The runners, thought to be messengers, carry small white bags in their outstretched hands, and their bird beaks and eyes are sheathed in gold. In a common Peruvian practice, the images are reversed from one frontal to the other, producing a pleasing symmetry when the ornaments are worn.

Hat Badge. The central part of this stunning medallion was fabricated in France about 1400–1410. Made of gold, it has been enameled in fine detail. The angels' wings of a fiery red extend to protect the heads of those below. Touched with green, the twisted crown of thorns is being removed by an angel. The fabric across the foreground has been decorated with blue flowers. The frame, made about 1550 in France or Germany, has been embellished with black enamel and set with diamonds. Two hoops for attachment are visible on the upper half of the frame.

Hat Badge. While this badge gained its initial reputation as a work of Ghiberti commissioned by Cosimo de'Medici, it is probably of a later date—the second half of the fifteenth century. This fact does not detract from its value as an exciting example of superb Renaissance craftsmanship. It charmingly depicts in high relief Saint John the Evangelist in a forest with the Lamb of Christ, the emblem used by the Wool Guild of Florence. The leafy frame has been accented with pearls and table-cut gems.

Portrait of a Man. Hat badges originated in the Middle Ages as humble objects made of lead or pewter. They served as devotional objects worn to show evidence of a pilgrimage or as a badge to display one's allegiance. The religious badges were made and sold at pilgrimage sites. Although sometimes constructed as brooches so that they could be pinned to the upturned brim of a hat, generally they had hoops or holes that permitted them to be sewn on. Gradually they became more and more ornate, losing their religious significance and evolving into one of the most flamboyant pieces of secular jewelry worn during the Renaissance. People began asking artists to execute unique designs for them. Benvenuto Cellini describes how in 1524 he created the most beautiful gold *enseignes* in bas relief. Eventually, the badge evolved into the aigrette, a gem-studded feather holder. Aigrettes, too, became more grandiose, and by the middle of the seventeenth century were incorporating huge plumes. The nobleman in this portrait by Quentin Massys (Flemish, 1465/66–1530) wears three badges on his hat. They are indecipherable, but judging from their plain appearance, we might assume that they are the pilgrimage badges of a religious man, especially since he also wears a gold chain with a crucifix. Two rings are worn on the hand in which he holds a sword whose handle is embellished with black enamel and a pearl. In this portrait we clearly see the artist's special interest in jewelry.

Pendant. In the first several centuries of the Christian era, the cross was a clandestine symbol used by the persecuted adherents of the new religion. After his mother, Saint Helena, claimed she had discovered the true cross in 326, the Roman Emperor Constantine acknowledged the cross as the public symbol of Christianity. By the Middle Ages, the cross was used in its smallest, most private form as a personal devotional object and in its largest manifestation as the architectural configuration of cathedrals. This gold cross with diamonds set in high collets surrounded by enameled flowers and vines was made in Germany between 1550 and 1575.

Male Figure. This statue of brass was cast in the seventeenth century by artists of the Court of Benin, a vast kingdom that thrived from the thirteenth century until the end of the nineteenth in what is now southern Nigeria. The figure's cross pendant has prompted several interpretations of his identity, and it even led early Portuguese visitors to believe they had found the legendary Christian realm of Prestor John. The cross is one of the emblems of authority delivered to a new Oba, or king, to show the approval of the ruler of Ife, a kingdom from which the Benin royal family traces its descent. Crosses are also worn by priests of the Benin creator god, and by palace officials who perform rituals recalling the origin of the dynasty. The art of lost-wax casting was introduced to the kingdom in the late fourteenth century, but artists were allowed to create work only for the king. The court possessed a magnificent collection that, tragically, was seized and dispersed.

Necklace. Discovered on the island of Cyprus, this Byzantine necklace was probably fabricated in Constantinople during the second half of the sixth or the beginning of the seventh century. The necklace combines amphorae, usually associated with the cult of Dionysos, with a Christian cross, here flanked by leaf-shaped pendants similar in shape to the cypress trees that often flank the cross in Byzantine representations. Strung between each pendant are beads produced by a technique known as *opus interrasile*, in which a sheet of metal is perforated to create an openwork pattern. Byzantine jewelers formed the sheets into tubes, soldering the seams to create beads.

A Member of the vom Rhein Family. The origin of the Christian rosary is uncertain, but an early record exists in Lady Godiva's bequest to a convent she founded in the eleventh century of a string of jewels that she used to count her prayers. The form of these circlets evolved over several centuries. Large beads for saying the Our Father were consequently called "paternoster beads," and smaller beads used for counting Hail Marys were called "ave beads." Guilds of prayer-bead jewelers were active by the thirteenth century, and they were called "paternosters," like their strings of beads. By the fifteenth century these beads were in great demand. They were worn as necklaces and hung from belts, not only as a show of religious devotion but also as an accompaniment to fashionable dress. Many were made from precious materials, such as amber, coral, jet, pearl, garnet, and gold. Some beads were made in the form of a pomander ball with musk or cloves inside. In this portrait by Conrad Faber von Creuznach (German, act. by 1524–52/53), the sitter holds a rosary of jet beads that terminates in what appears to be a paternoster pomander made of enameled gold. The artist has applied gold leaf to the painting in order to highlight the man's cap, his ring, and the paternoster bead.

Rosary Bead. The center of boxwood carving was in Flanders, where this magnificent bead was made during the sixteenth century, the work of a highly accomplished craftsman. The dense and regular grain of the wood made it particularly suitable for small-scale carvings. When opened, the upper capsule forms a triptych. This bead was most likely a component of a complete rosary.

Jan, First Count of Egmond
(1438–1516). This portrait by
the Master of Alkmaar (Dutch,
act. about 1504) was probably
painted shortly before the sitter's death. He wears the Order
of the Golden Fleece, which was
granted to him in 1491 by Philip
the Fair of Burgundy. The order
was created in 1430 by Philip the
Good in honor of his marriage
and at first was bestowed on only
twenty-four knights. Twenty-four
collars, like the one worn in this
portrait, were made by the Bruges
goldsmith Jean Peutin. Eventually, members of the order increased,
and some knights commissioned
the making of their own collars
and badges. Some were quite
lavish, with large diamonds and
rubies that displayed wealth as
well as honor.

**Général Etienne-Maurice
Gérard, Marshal of France.**
When this portrait was painted
in 1816, both the sitter and the artist, Jacques-Louis David (French,
1748–1825), were in exile in
Brussels following Napoleon's
1815 defeat at Waterloo. Etienne-
Maurice, comte de Gérard, had a
distinguished career in the French
army. A volunteer at eighteen in
1791, he was made a baron by
Napoleon after the battle of
Wagram, held the rank of general
of division during the Russian
campaign, and was named count
of the Empire in 1813. Louis XVIII
awarded him the Legion of Honor
and the Knighthood of Saint
Louis in 1814. During the Hundred Days Napoleon named him
Peer of France. As in so many portraits of monarchs who sought to
demonstrate their greatness by
wearing court jewels, we can read
the proud history of the man in his
decorated uniform. However,
because of the painter's genius in
seeing beneath the ostentation, he
also evokes the character of this
aging soldier in a distinguished
and restrained portrait.

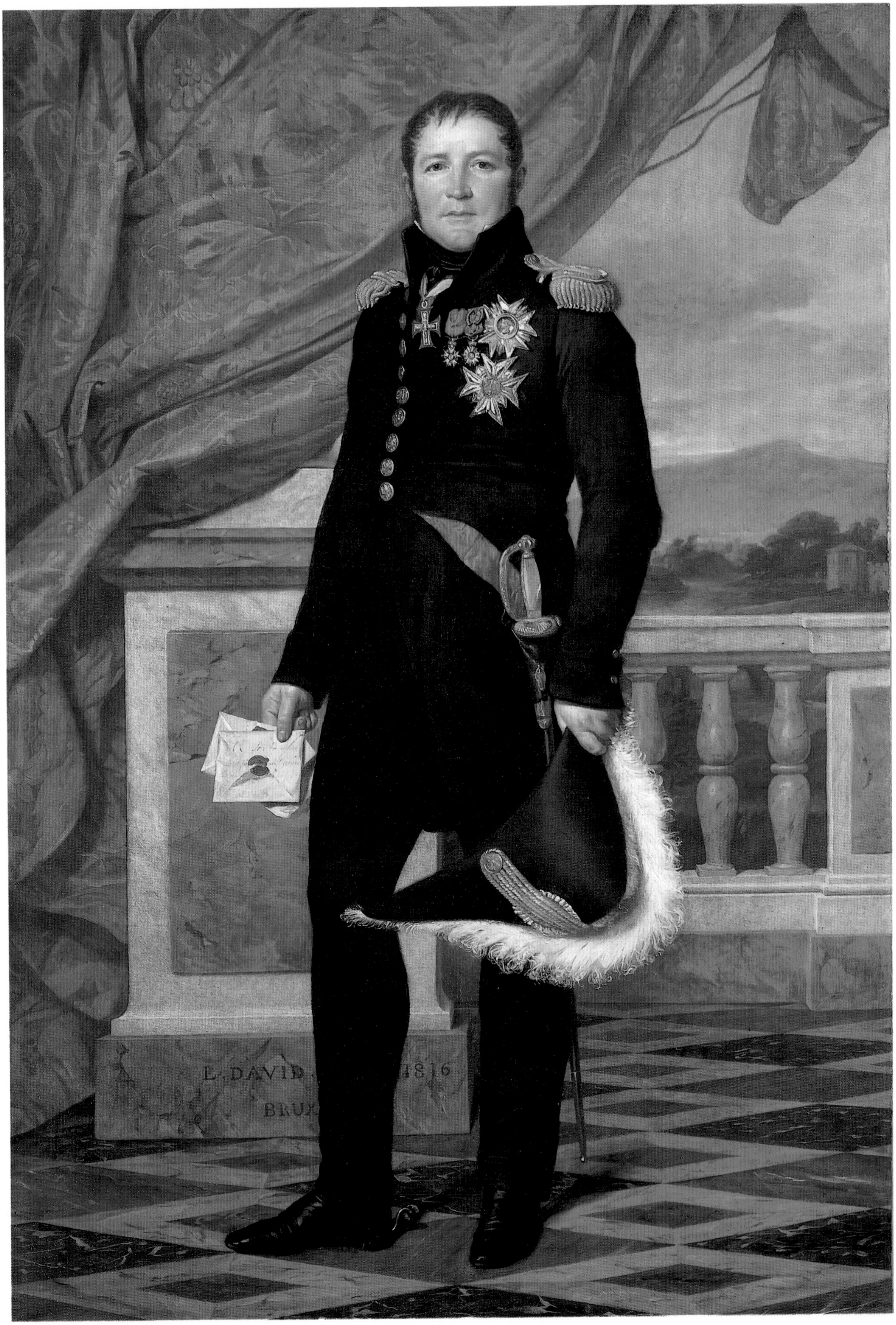
L. DAVID
1816

Pectoral. Neck rings are recorded in early sources as playing a role both in the glorification of military heroes and in coronation ceremonies. This impressive pectoral necklace is composed of a simple hollow neck ring attached to a frame that is set with a large medallion flanked by coins and two small decorative nielloed disks. Although it was found in Egypt, the pectoral is believed to have been made in Constantinople during the middle of the sixth century. A personification of that city is depicted on the reverse of the central medallion. The front of the medallion and the smaller coins depict Byzantine emperors. The two ribbed rings at the pectoral's lower edge once held a large medallion of the emperor Theodosius I. This imperial imagery suggests that the pectoral comprises several military trophies that once belonged to a distinguished general or a member of the imperial court.

Necklace. The gold beads of this reconstructed necklace were made in northern Peru between the third and the sixth centuries when that area was ruled by the Moche. The pattern on the beads depicts a frog clutching the necks of the two-headed snake that encircles it. Originally all the beads would have been set with stone inlay, probably chrysocolla or turquoise; the present inlay in the center bead is a modern replacement. The beads are hollow, and some of them contain a pellet, which creates a sound when the necklace is shaken. Buried in a grave long before the arrival of the Conquistadors, this powerfully beautiful necklace escaped the destruction wrought when the Spanish appropriated, exported, and melted down vast quantities of the goldwork of Precolumbian civilizations.

Fudō Myō-ō. This wooden Japanese statue represents a guardian of the faith who protects the Buddha from enemies with his sword of wisdom and captures evil forces with his lasso. The restrained, gentle curves of the figure are typical of the sculpture created in Japan during the twelfth century. The flat openwork necklace of gilt with accents of tiny colored beads was probably added at a later date. The necklace is not simply decorative. A wheel, which symbolizes the first preaching by Buddha, has been incorporated into the scrolling pattern of lotus, which is also a Buddhist symbol for purity, rising as it does from a muddy pond. Like the religion itself, the practice of adorning representations of Buddhist deities with jewelry originated in India.

Judith with the Head of Holofernes. "And she washed her body, and anointed herself with the best ointment, and plaited the hair of her head, and put a bonnet upon her head, and clothed herself with the garments of her gladness; and put sandals on her feet, and took her bracelets, and lilies and earlets and rings and adorned herself with all her ornaments" (Judith 10:3). In this sumptuous apparel the radiant Judith went forth to save her Jewish people from the siege of Holofernes. So captivated by her beauty that he unwittingly dismissed his servants, Holofernes gave Judith the opportunity to behead him in his drunken sleep. Lucas Cranach the Elder (German, 1472–1553) followed the biblical passage describing Judith's attire but adorned her in clothing and jewels of the 1530s when this painting was made. Numerous gold rings set with jewels can be seen on Judith's fingers through the slits of her sheer gloves. Her hair is held in a golden net adorned with pearls in a pattern that matches the one on her bodice. A choker of gold is studded with a profusion of emeralds, rubies, and pearls. Massive gold chains were immensely popular in both Flanders and Germany at this time, and Cranach often portrayed women wearing little else. He was one of the most versatile and prolific artists of the Northern Renaissance, a humanist who preferred mythological and classical subjects to religious ones.

Reliquary Bust. Vessels containing sacred remains were sometimes designed in the shape of the relic they housed, and a special devotion to reliquaries in bust form containing the skulls of local saints developed in the region of Limoges during the Middle Ages. This reliquary bust was fabricated there between 1220 and 1240 and once held the skull of Saint Yrieix, a local churchman of the sixth century. The sumptuous materials used to construct the reliquary reflect its importance. The artist has also used a number of techniques from the jeweler's repertoire—repoussé, chasing, filigree, casting, riveting, and lapidary. The silver-gilt sheets of beaten metal were set over a wooden core, which is sculpted to a high degree of finish. The reflective polished surface of this precious sculpture made it an imposing image, whether set on an altar surrounded by flickering candlelight or carried in open-air processions.

Madonna and Child with Angels.
In a costume devoid of other jewelry, the Virgin has fastened her cloak with a magnificent clasp. Surrounded by a decorative gold frame and four large crystal spheres, the central rectangular crystal is placed in a quatrefoil setting similar to those on the necklaces worn by Judith on the previous page. Crystal spheres also accent the elements attached directly to the cloak. The use of various devices to hold clothing in place is an ancient one. Clasps were especially necessary when clothing was a contrived arrangement of long pieces of fabric with no seams. As with other utilitarian objects, the need to make a functional fastener was overtaken by the desire to make a beautiful one. In this painting Cosimo Rosselli (Italian, 1439–1507) has depicted an object so lovely that we may not notice its function at first glance.

Clasp. On the right side of this magnificent gilt-bronze buckle, a crowned man rests his feet on a lion; at the left a veiled woman places her feet on a basilisk, a mythical beast whose monkey head tops the body of a dragon. Each figure is accompanied by an attendant, and the group is arranged within an acanthus-vine framework. Although the identity of the figures is uncertain, the creatures suggest a depiction of Psalm 91:13: "Thou shalt tread upon the adder and the basilisk and trample under foot the lion and the dragon." The small figures, with their finely articulated drapery, are cast in high relief, which gives them a sense of monumentality that typifies the style pioneered by the late-twelfth-century Mosan goldsmith Nicholas of Verdun. The holes for attaching the clasp are visible but the fastening mechanism has been disguised within the artistic composition.

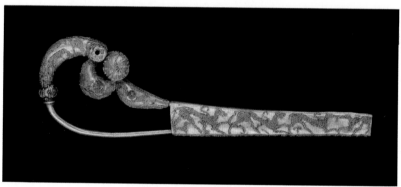

Fibula. One of the earliest devices for securing draped fabric clothing was the fibula, a precursor of the modern safety pin, which was already in common use in Minoan Crete by 1300 B.C.. Through the centuries into the Middle Ages, the fibula was used by many cultures, each creating or borrowing different forms of construction and decoration. Bows were enhanced and made larger to accommodate more material; catches and springs were also imaginatively garnished. The Etruscans elaborated magnificently on the basic fibula form in this masterpiece of the seventh century B.C. Using their unparalleled mastery of granulation, they have embellished the catch with a parade of animals each composed of minute grains of gold. Also adorned with granulation, the bow and the spring mechanism represent a continuous, graciously curving form.

Oval Brooch. This bronze Viking brooch from the tenth century would have been one of a pair used by a woman to fasten her shoulder strap to the front of her tunic. The brooch is made in two parts: a gilt base and a convex cast gilt openwork top. The outer shell is cast with five large hollow bosses protruding from the dome, and fine silver wings probably once decorated the now-empty pairs of holes. The dome and the projecting ornaments on the shell have been enhanced by abstract animal-style motifs cast in a technique known as "chip-carving" because of its resemblance to woodworking. Only traces of the gilding on the upper part of the brooch have survived. The geographical distribution of these unique brooches attest to the widespread influence of the Vikings. Examples have been found in Ireland, England, Scotland, France, and Russia.

The Annunciation. Hans Memling (Flemish, act. by 1465–d. 1494) was born in Germany but spent most of his life in Bruges, where he was a prolific and very popular artist. One of the most engaging aspects of Flemish religious art is its use of ordinary contemporary backgrounds for momentous biblical events. In this painting, one of Memling's masterworks dating from about 1482, the setting is the comfortably bourgeois home of a Bruges merchant, stocked with the artifacts of everyday life. The Virgin's pure white dress is discreetly trimmed in gold bands set with pearls and gems, and the Archangel wears an elaborate cope woven with red and gold thread. It is held in place by a gold morse, a large clasp used with this particular ecclesiastical garment. Four cabochon gems (two rubies and two sapphires) and four pearls encircle a point-cut diamond. Developed in the fourteenth century, the point cut is an octahedron crystal (think of two pyramids connected base-to-base), all eight sides of which have been polished. It was the first in a series of steps that eventually led over several centuries to today's familiar brilliant cut. Except for the round cabochon emeralds and pearls, the gems in the base of the Archangel's crown are also point cut.

Morse. This octalobular plaque of copper gilt and enamel represents Saint Francis of Assisi receiving the stigmata, the five wounds of the crucified Christ. The scene takes place at night with the crescent moon and stars shining in the sky. The original deep sapphire-blue sky has darkened with age, but the vibrant red enamels and gilt surfaces lend drama to the depiction of this miracle. The plaque was created in Tuscany during the first half of the fourteenth century, two hundred years after the death of Saint Francis. He was said to be dwelling in a hermitage when he received the stigmata in September of 1224. The reverse of the morse has the remains of the attachments designed to affix it to the neck of a liturgical vestment. Like the morse in the painting, this example is quite large, measuring 4½ inches in diameter.

Portrait of a Man and a Woman at a Casement. Fra Filippo Lippi (Italian, ca. 1406–69) has placed a magnificent brooch in a prominent position in this painting and carefully directed our attention to it with the man's pointing finger, the line of the woman's headdress, and the top of her sleeve. Set in gold and surrounded by four crystal spheres is a remarkable table-cut stone. This innovative cut originated in the early fifteenth century, shortly before 1440, about the time this painting was completed. The new technique enhanced the natural brilliance of stones to a remarkable degree. In the table cut, the top part of an octahedral crystal is removed, creating a "table." Undoubtedly, this innovative jewel was highly prized by its owner, possibly Angiola di Bernardo Sapiti. This panel may commemorate her marriage to Lorenzo di Ranieri Scolari (1407–78), the man in the window who holds the arms of his Florentine family. Both sitters wear multiple rings. She is fashionably dressed in the French style *(alla parigina)*, with the partially hidden word "Leal[ta]" (fidelity), embroidered in gold and embellished with pearls on her sleeve. Her simple pearl necklace complements the trim on her headdress, which is encrusted with seed pearls and other gems.

Nono (Mademoiselle Lebasque). Henri Matisse (French, 1869–1954) had reason to take special interest in the sitter, for not only was she the daughter of his friend Henri Lebasque, but she was also the first girlfriend of his son, Pierre. Painted about 1908, the portrait shows Mlle Lebasque wearing a brooch of large silver balls pinned to the high ruff of her dress. Given her youth and modest daytime attire, she has selected an appropriately unpretentious but lovely adornment.

Brooch. This glorious brooch of diamonds set in gold, with accents in black enamel, is attributed to Léon Rouvenat (French, 1809–74), although it lacks the identifying mark of the firm. The design and technique are very similar to the jewels shown by him at the Universal Exhibition in Paris in 1867. Thirty-eight of the jewels exhibited there were acquired by the Viceroy of Egypt. The engraved inscription on the back indicates this piece may have been one of them. The jewel can be worn in two ways: as a brooch, fastened by a pin, or as a belt ornament, attached by two long vertical hooks, which are slipped over the edge of a band of fabric.

Christ Blessing, Surrounded by a Donor and His Family. One of the widespread fashions of the early sixteenth century was the wearing of large, heavy chains. In England Henry VIII gave them as presents to ambassadors and as rewards to men who had rendered a service to the crown. Men also wore them in France. In Flanders and Germany, however, they were mostly worn by women. It has not been possible to identify the austere devout family represented in this triptych attributed to Ludger tom Ring the Younger (German, 1522–84), but their ages are inscribed on the wall above their heads. As piously dour as the mother and her two daughters may appear, they are nonetheless quite fashionably attired. Each wears a large gold chain and cinches her dress with a woven belt bearing an ornate gold buckle. Multiple rings can be seen on the exposed hands. Cloak brooches were old-fashioned by this time, so only the historically attired figure of Christ wears one. The new style is represented by the lovely pendant displayed by the daughter on the right (detail on page 27), who wears it suspended from an ornate chain of openwork flat links.

Saint Catherine of Alexandria. A legendary fourth-century martyr and one of the most popular saints of the medieval church, Saint Catherine is shown here holding the spiked wheel upon which she was tortured. This *ronde-bosse* enameled statuette is reputed to have come from a convent in Clermont-Ferrand; the fine workmanship, sensitive modeling, and precious gem-studded decoration are more consistent with the finest works produced in Paris for royal and aristocratic patrons around 1400. The image may have come from a reliquary, where it and figures of other saints would have been integrated into an architectural ensemble. Enameling *en ronde bosse* is a technique for applying enamel on a round figure, as has been done here, or on a raised piece like the hat badge on page 64. Saint Catherine's brooch is a miniature version of the cluster brooches worn during the fourteenth century.

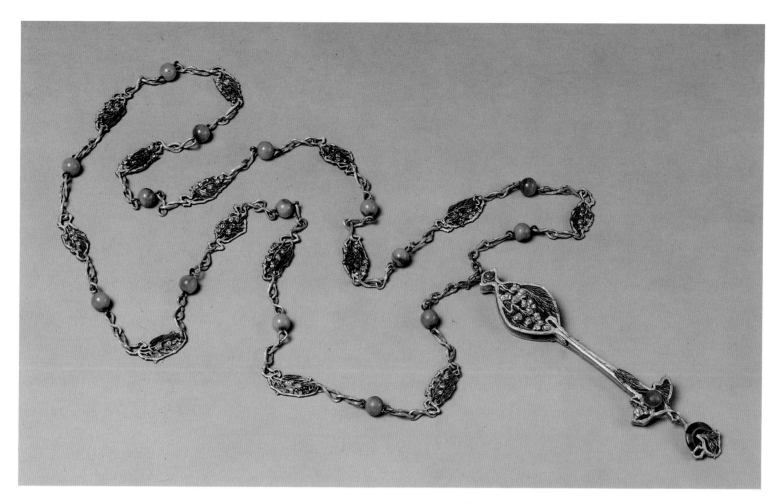

Lorgnette and Chain. When René Lalique (French, 1860–1945) made this piece at the turn of the twentieth century, lorgnettes were frequently illustrated in fashion plates. The exquisite 33½-inch-long chain contains three elements: green-veined jade beads, openwork plaques of gold with white enamel vines whose green enamel *plique à jour* leaves surround flowers set with sparks of diamonds, and twisted links of gold again traced with white enamel. The lorgnette is designed with the same materials and motif. The eyeglasses are attached to a swivel in the oval section at the end of the long, graceful handle.

Portrait of a Woman. The greatest Dutch painter of the seventeenth century was Rembrandt van Rijn (Dutch, 1606–69). This portrait is one of a pair depicting an upper-middle-class couple, probably of Amsterdam. The paintings are both dated 1632, the date Rembrandt is thought to have moved to Amsterdam. Although the sitter's costume is dominated by her starched lace-trimmed ruff and wide cuffs, she still manages to display a fair amount of jewelry, as befits her station. Triple-strand bracelets of pearls are worn on each wrist. A gleaming ornament adorns her hair, and a discreet earring is barely visible. A fan with an ornate handle hangs fashionably by a chain from her belt. She also wears a beautiful chain around her shoulders in which black melon-shaped beads are connected by intricate gold links.

Louis Gueymard as Robert le Diable. In this portrait Gustave Courbet (French, 1819–77) depicts the tenor Gueymard in the title role of Meyerbeer's opera *Robert le Diable.* Wearing a massive gold chain, which symbolizes the power of worldly temptations, Robert sings "Oui, l'or est une chimère" (Yes, gold is a chimera) as he begins to play dice with servants of the devil.

Madame Jacques-Louis Leblanc (Françoise Poncelle). Jean-Auguste-Dominique Ingres (French, 1780–1867) first met the Leblancs in Florence, probably in 1820 when Madame Leblanc was lady-in-waiting to Napoleon's sister, the grand duchess of Tuscany. Ingres painted this portrait and one of Madame Leblanc's husband in 1823. She wears very plain rings, and her hoop earrings, each set with a small diamond, are barely visible. Her most prominent piece of jewelry is a watch worn on a long chain around her neck and also secured to her belt. The small round catch on the chain is studded with small turquoises matching those on the watch and hook-plate. In what appears to be an afterthought, but given its magnificence could not have been, she has placed her diamond *rivière* on her lap. Neither the watch on its long chain nor the *rivière* were innovative fashion statements in 1823, as both had been worn for some time. Perhaps an article published in a French fashion journal in 1821 stating that diamond *rivières* should now be worn only by dowagers prompted Madame Leblanc to show but not wear her impressive diamonds.

Watch and Châtelaine. In the eighteenth century the châtelaine was the most predominant type of jewelry worn during the daytime. It consisted of three main parts: an ornamental hook-plate that was attached to the belt, a number of chains affixed to the plate, and objects attached to the dangling ends of each chain. Large châtelaines were portable workshops with keys, needle cases, scissors, rulers, compasses, and even little notebooks. This châtelaine, made in Germany between 1750 and 1775, is crafted of gold and carnelian and, most unusually for this type of jewelry, is set with precious gems. Although some châtelaines have as many as nine chains, this one has three extraordinarily decorative ones terminating in a watch, a seal, and a watch key. Gold was not the only material used for châtelaines; many were made of pinchbeck, copper gilt, and even steel. They remained in fashion for well over a century.

Watch. In the early stages of their evolution watches were incredibly unreliable. The seventeenth-century watch was used more to display one's sophistication than for the accurate keeping of time. Consequently, they were worn so that they could be seen and admired. The cases, then, became the vehicle for some of the most imaginative and beautiful enamel work ever created. They were valued so highly that when watchmaking technology improved, some owners had replacement watches made to fit the original cases. The movement of this elegant watch was made in Paris around 1650 by Josias Goullons. The enamelwork on the dial, the rim, and the inside of the cover depict tiny figures in pleasant landscapes. The back of the case and the exterior of the cover are painted with scenes of the Holy Family with Saint John and the Virgin and Child with Saint John.

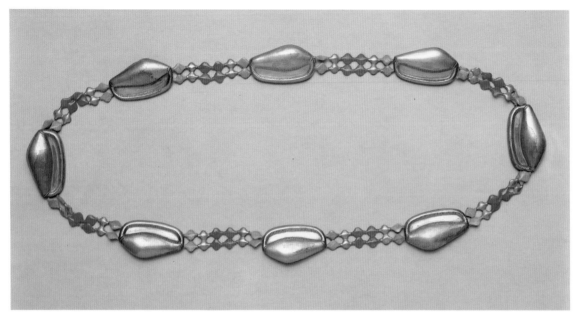

mounts, which are twice the size shown here, are typical of their personal ornaments.

Girdle. This superb gold belt fabricated from Byzantine medallions and coins dates from the beginning of the seventh century and is probably from Constantinople. Most of the coins and all of the medallions were given by the Emperor Maurice Tiberius in commemoration of his assumption of the consulship for the first time in 583 and then again in 602. The recipient had these gifts made into this belt. Unlike the coins used in most jewelry at that time, some of the coins in this girdle were rare when the belt was made.

Cowrie Girdle. This splendid girdle was worn by the same princess who owned the bracelet reproduced on the endpapers in this book. Constructed during the eighteenth century B.C., it is composed of eight hollow gold cowrie shells, one of which serves as a clasp. Beads of gold, carnelian, and green feldspar shaped like acacia seeds separate the shells. The cowries contain metal pellets, which would tinkle seductively as the princess walked.

Katharina Merian. While they are ultimately utilitarian objects, belts do change with fashion and during some eras have become highly decorative. This portrait attributed to Hans Brosamer (German, act. by 1536–d. 1552?) was completed when the melancholy-looking sitter was thirty-eight. Her hands have been carefully placed so that her admirable belt can be seen. Relieving the stark black dress, it has a plain buckle and is punctuated with gleaming gold studs.

Gold Mounts. The Avars, a coalition of two defeated armies, the Jouan Jouan and the White Huns, became a powerful migratory force during the sixth and seventh centuries. Constantly on the move and at war, they sensibly invested their wealth in portable, wearable objects. The foliate forms and animal motifs of these powerfully elegant gold belt

Buckle. This extraordinarily beautiful gold Hunnish belt buckle is a miniature masterpiece. The design is created with thin, perfectly cut garnets that have been set over patterned gold foil. The buckle was made in the first half of the fifth century, a time when Attila ruled (433–53) and when the Huns were so feared by the Romans that they paid a yearly tribute ranging from 350 to 700 pounds of gold.

Elijah Boardman. During the eighteenth century, buckles became very important items of daytime jewelry. It was no longer fashionable for men to flaunt their status with extravagant jewels, so the vehicle of their display became the buckle and the button. These were produced in materials to fit every pocketbook, from the courtier's diamonds set in gold to the ordinary man's cut steel and paste. As the century progressed, the size of these buckles and buttons increased. Ralph Earl (American, 1751–1801) painted this young merchant in 1789. Pictured in his place of business, Mr. Boardman wears a costume reflecting an exceptional knowledge of current British style, unusual for a resident of Connecticut at that time. In addition to his fancy buttons and buckles, a watch on a gold chain hangs from his belt.

Mr. and Mrs. I. N. Phelps Stokes. John Singer Sargent (American, 1856–1925) painted this couple in 1897, two years after they were married. Very sporting with her boater and bow tie, Mrs. Stokes displays a taste for elegance by wearing a silver openwork belt buckle. The 1859 discovery of the Comstock Lode in Nevada had added vast amounts of silver to the world market. Within a decade, the wearing of silver was very fashionable, especially during the daytime. Mr. Stokes has recalled that Sargent was especially proud of the "spiral stroke with which he produced the diamond in Edith's engagement ring."

Nephrite Belt Hook. Because jade is such a tough stone, the craftsman who carved this fine piece was able to utilize it for the demanding task of holding a belt. Made in the Chinese style in Northern India in the late nineteenth century, this belt hook of fine translucent nephrite has been inlaid with gold and set with rubies, diamonds, and rock crystals placed over green foil to imitate emeralds.

Belt Buckle. This depiction of two felines biting the necks of two ibexes, whose legs are folded under their bellies, was made late in the first millennium B.C. in the eastern Steppes, on the northern border of China. It features bold images of animals, full of life and movement, typical of nomadic art. Cast from gold, this was probably one of a pair of plaques used as a belt buckle.

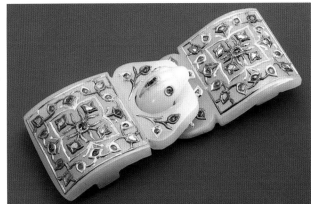

Armbands. The beginning of the Hellenistic period is conventionally dated to 323 B.C., the year of the death of Alexander the Great. His conquests, which extended as far as India, dramatically widened the horizon of the Greek world, introducing new types of subject matter, new materials, and new sources of wealth. This pair of armlets from the third century B.C. is made of one of those materials: gold. The spiral bracelet enjoyed a very long history in the Greek world, and here the form has been used to portray Triton, the son of Poseidon and a sea god. He has been provided with a female counterpart, and they are each represented with a human body which is transformed into the tail of a fish below the waist and ends in the shape of a serpent. Both the Triton and the Tritoness carry Erotes, aspects of the god of love, often depicted as a winged youth.

Salomé. This picture began as a study of the head of a young peasant whom Henri Regnault (French, 1843–71) met in the Roman campagna in 1869. Later he added canvas to three sides of the painting and painted the complete figure, as we see it, adding the final touches when he was in Tangier in 1870. He considered several titles *(Esclave Favorite* and *Poetassa de Cordoba)* before adopting *Salomé,* which is particularly appropriate because the figure holds the knife and basin associated with the beheading of Saint John the Baptist. On her upper arm Salome wears a sinister snake bracelet, the head set with a pink stone. The hoop bracelet in the form of a serpent is an ancient motif, popular in Egypt, Greece, and Rome. The bracelet of the sitter, though appropriate for the period in which Salome danced, was also a fashionable ornament of the period when the painting was made.

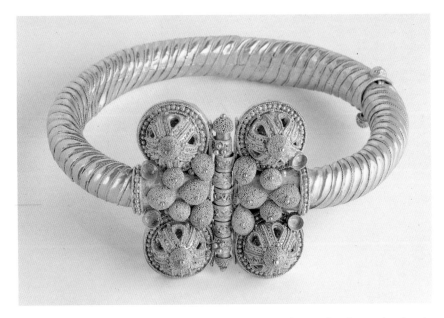

Armlet. One of a pair, this gorgeous armlet is a pivotal piece for the study of early medieval jewelry in Greater Iran. Each of the four hemispheres flanking the clasp sits on a flat disk of thin gold. The disks were decorated by embossing them over a relatively new coin bearing the name of the Abbasid caliph al-Qadir Bilah (991–1031), which enables us to date this piece to the first half of the eleventh century. The hollow hoop has been fabricated from gold sheet and decorated with twisted wire. The extravagant clasp is richly embellished with fine granulation; the empty collets would have been set with stones. Both the use of simulated coins and the twisted shank are pre-Islamic jewelry forms, indicating the continued conservatism and traditionalism of the jeweler's art.

Armband Centerpiece. When it was made originally in Northern India between the seventeenth and nineteenth centuries, this gold piece was set with two cabochon emeralds, numerous rubies, and large colorless sapphires. In the late 1920s or 1930s the firm of Cartier in Paris converted the piece to a brooch and added the brilliant-cut diamonds, which are set in silver or platinum, and the pearls and two black beads on the outer edges. If these added elements were to disappear, you could see the armband in its pristine form. A chain or cord would have held the piece in place on the upper arm.

The Buddha Amoghasiddhi Attended by Bodhisattvas. This *thanka,* or painting on cloth, was painted in Tibet during the first half of the thirteenth century. It portrays the transcendental Buddha Amoghasiddhi in his northern paradise attended by bodhisattvas. Typical of these cosmic buddhas, but unusual for buddhas in general, he is richly adorned with lavish jewelry. His bracelets, anklets, and necklaces of gold are set with precious gems. His hair is piled up in a tall chignon and dressed with a jeweled tiara and numerous precious ornaments. The armbands have a large triangular element, like those of the tiara, affixed to an armband from which dangle gold chains, some in the form of swags, others ending in tassels. Smaller jeweled triangular elements are attached to the sides of the band. A profusion of other jewelry—earplugs, necklaces, bangles, anklets, and a belt—complete his parure. The profusion of jewelry denotes that the *sambhogakaya,* the "reflected" form taken by enlightened ones in their heavens, is being represented. The size of each figure reflects the degree of their spiritual perfection. Amoghasiddhi, therefore, is represented as comparatively enormous, while a small monk is portrayed in the lower righthand corner. This *thanka* would have been part of a set of five celestial Buddhas, and it is probable that the monk officiated at the ceremony during which the set was consecrated. He may actually have been its donor as well.

Pair of Armlets. These colorful, gleaming armlets were made in Egypt during the early Eighteenth Dynasty between about 1545 and 1525 B.C. They contain small beads of gold, bronze or copper, carnelian, green faience or glass, blue glass, and lapis lazuli strung in seven rows. As with the bracelet illustrated on the endpapers, each strand is held in position by strategically placed gold spacer beads. One is clearly visible just to the left of the carnelian beads in the bracelet on the left. Although the appearance is that of a vertical line of gold beads, it is actually a solid piece with seven holes.

Coffin Lid. The coffins of Amenemope, a member of a priestly Theban family during the late Twenty-first to early Twenty-second Dynasty (ca. 950–850 B.C.), are masterpieces of colorful detail and stylized religious design. This powerful painting on the inside of the cover represents Amenhotpe I, the first king of Dynasty 18. He wears the Blue Crown, and his body is draped in a beaded tunic. Both the pharaoh and the Nile gods that flank him are richly adorned with broad collars, armlets, and bracelets. The cartouches on the jewelry of the pharaoh, similar to those on the inside of the bracelets to the right, are inscribed with the name of the god Osiris.

Pair of Bracelets. The treasure of three minor wives of Tuthmosis III, of which these bracelets are a part, represents the most spectacular trove of royal jewelry from Dynasty 18 prior to the reign of Tutankhamun. Made between about 1480 and 1450 B.C., the hinged bracelets are fashioned of gold, beaten to shape, burnished to a high gloss, and inlaid with alternating cylindrical pieces of turquoise, carnelian, and a third unidentified substance, possibly glass. Inscribed on the interior with the royal titles of Tuthmosis III, they are skillfully chased so that the broad grooves reflect light brilliantly. The bracelets were apparently intended to be worn as a matched pair.

Two Gold Bracelets. These bracelets are actually a matching pair. Each one is a *naoratna,* or nine-gem jewel, a talismanic combination that is recorded in ancient Hindu treatises about gems. The top bracelet shows the side that is set with pearl, coral, diamond, emerald, ruby, chrysoberyl, sapphire, topaz, and turquoise. The tenth stone is an additional diamond. The ruby represents the sun, and the other stones represent the four cardinal and four intercardinal points of the universe. The wearer was thought to be protected through the incorporation of every astrological influence. Less opulent, but equally charming, the other side of these bracelets is decorated with a quatrefoil pattern in white and green enamel. The bracelets were made in Northern India between the seventeenth and nineteenth centuries, and similar ones are still made in India today.

Pair of Bracelets. These striking crystal and gold bangles are part of the Ganymede treasure named after the earrings illustrated on page 61. Found sometime before 1913, this trove contains some of the finest pieces of northern Greek jewelry known. Carved from rock crystal, the hoops of these bracelets are grooved and embellished with fine gold wire. The gold terminals are in the form of confronted rams' heads, their elongated necks decorated with a profusion of designs rendered in filigree. In addition to these bracelets and the earrings already discussed, the Ganymede group includes a gold necklace, an emerald ring, and four gold fibulae. The woman who owned this splendidly rich parure in the late fourth century B.C. was obviously beautifully adorned.

L'Espagnole: Harmonie en bleu. During the period 1911–13, Henri Matisse visited North Africa three times. His experiences there had a profound influence on his art throughout his career. The intriguing figure of the odalisque preoccupied the artist during the 1920s, when he painted the figure in various exotic settings. The woman in this painting from 1923 is not dressed as an odalisque but, with her mantilla and fan, as a Spanish lady. The flowing mantilla serves as a link between the geometric pattern of the tabletop and the profusion of soft, full flowers behind her. While not ornate, the massive gold and silver bangles, the many finger rings, and the prominent necklace of large beads complement the exotic atmosphere that Matisse has created.

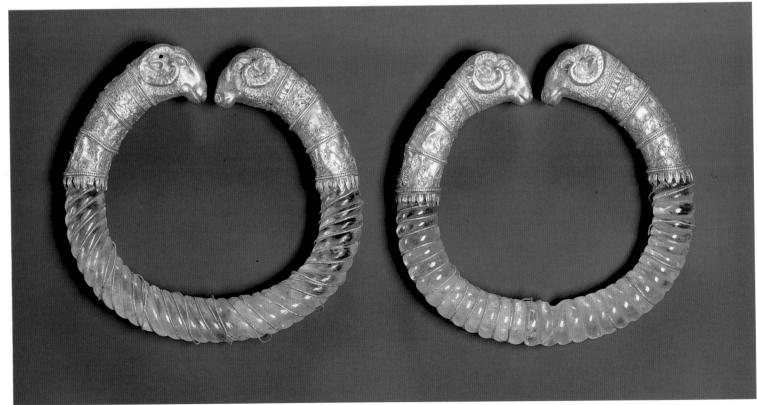

DA·ICH·HET·DIE·GE
STALT·WAS·ICH·ZZ·
IAR·ALT·1517·HH
PINCEBAT·

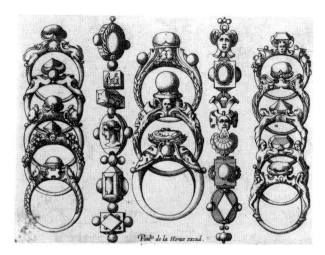

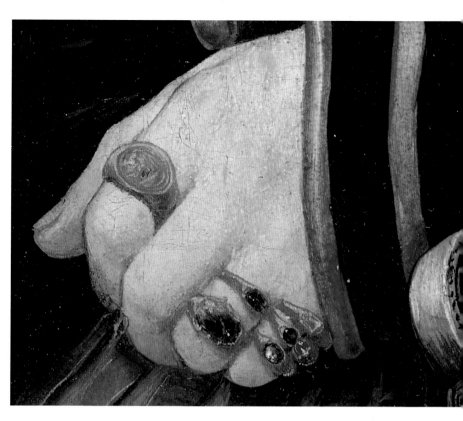

Benedikt von Hertenstein. In 1517, while in Lucerne on a commission to create frescoes for a mansion recently built by the mayor, the young Hans Holbein also painted this portrait of the mayor's son, who had just been elected to the city council. The inscription on the wall at the left translates: "When I looked like this I was 22 years old. 1517. H. H. painted it." The sitter is attired in a fashion that expresses wealth and privilege. He has accented his hat with glittering aglets, and placed a large, heavy chain around his neck. He wears six rings on his left hand, a detail of which appears above. Tragically, five years after the portrait was painted, this promising young man died at the Battle of Bicocca, where he was serving as a Swiss mercenary soldier.

Rings. Pictured above is one of twenty engravings that appear in a booklet of designs by René Boyvin (French, 1530?–98). Some of the complex construction and beautifully elaborate decoration of Renaissance rings can be seen in this single engraving. We know that the publication of jewelry designs changed the way some jewelers worked in that they copied the designs of others, but we can speculate that these engravings also changed the way clients shopped. In this engraving the client would see three rows of rings and two rows of links and, after reviewing the designs, would select a suitable setting for a gem or pearl. The ring at the bottom of the middle row is styled to be set with a cameo. Only after the choices were made would the ring be fabricated by the goldsmith. The buyer could similarly select one of the link designs, which would be made into a chain or bracelet. The engravings in Boyvin's booklet are unsigned and undated, bearing only the name of the publisher, Paul de la Houue, who worked around 1600 and must have acquired the metal plates after Boyvin's death.

Ring. This exquisite ring was made in Paris, probably between 1550 and 1560, and displays the extraordinary heights achieved during the Renaissance in the art of ring making. The shank is decorated with an elaborate strapwork ornament that has been highlighted with colorful enamels. The bezel of the ring holds a turquoise-blue glass relief portrait of Alexander the Great as Herakles. The relief is attached to a gold base enameled in black. The resulting effect mimics a cameo. The head is framed by curly locks and a lion-skin headdress, which is tied under the chin by the animal's front legs and paws. These are made of burnished and matte-finished gold applied to the glass relief. The lion's teeth are highlighted with white enamel.

Benedikt von Hertenstein (detail). During the Renaissance both men and women liked to wear a number of rings on each finger, including the thumb. All the rings on this young man's fourth and little fingers are set with stones: rubies, emeralds, and diamonds, and perhaps a large garnet and a topaz, each in a beautifully simple setting. The signet ring on the sitter's index finger bears the seal of the Hertenstein family. Although the first rings ever worn were probably purely decorative, the custom of wearing a ring engraved so it could be used as a seal is several thousand years old. Egyptian jewelers carved intaglios in stone about 1800 B.C. and by 1400 B.C. had perfected the art of engraving the solid gold bezel with a seal. The Greeks began using signet rings about 600 B.C. Signet rings of metal and stone were worn extensively by the Romans, and the Franks preserved this custom after the fall of the Empire. Later in the Middle Ages, heraldic devices were used on signet rings. During the Renaissance, as in the past, a seal was necessary for conducting business, so families like the Hertensteins continued to wear distinctive designs on their own signet rings.

Ring. A carnelian scarab engraved with the figure of Herakles is mounted on this gold swivel ring. Made by an Etruscan craftsman probably during the early fifth century B.C., it continues a tradition that can be traced back to the Egyptians in the second millennium. The swivel mounting allows the wearer to utilize the stone as a seal without forfeiting the amuletic image of the beetle, which originally symbolized immortality.

Gold Ring. Made in Greece during the fourth century B.C., this ring testifies to the ongoing importance of the Trojan War to artists and their patrons. The bezel shows the Trojan prophetess Cassandra seeking refuge at the statue of Athena, as the Greek warrior Ajax is about to seize her. Given the gift of prophecy by Apollo, Cassandra was cursed with not being believed after she spurned him. Consequently, her warning to her fellow Trojans not to take in the massive image of a horse offered by the Greeks went unheeded.

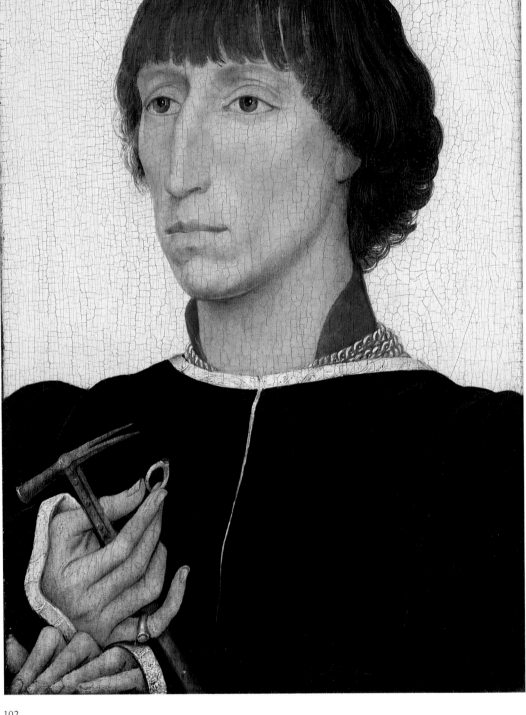

Francesco d'Este. The ritualized battles of the tournament were among the favorite activities enjoyed by courtiers in fifteenth-century Europe. Prizes were given for different events, and, according to one account, success at jousting was rewarded with a ruby ring. The subject of this portrait is the illegitimate son of Lionello d'Este, marquis of Ferrara. He was educated in the Burgundian court and spent most of his life there in the service of Philip the Good and Charles the Bold. He was about thirty when the Flemish artist Rogier van der Weyden painted this great masterpiece about 1460. The sitter's aristocratic bearing epitomizes the elegance of court society, and the hammer is connected with the tournament. We do not know but can surmise that the ruby ring he so proudly displays, in a way that the viewer cannot miss seeing it, was a prize won at a tournament.

Portrait of a Young Woman. Because it represents one of life's most important commitments, the simple gold wedding band is imbued with more emotion than any other form of jewelry. The sitter in this portrait by Lorenzo di Credi (Italian, 1459/60–1537) wears the black dress of a widow and holds her wedding ring in a tender gesture of remembrance.

Glossary

The numbers refer to the page where the term is first used in the text.

Aglets. Originally, the metal tips on the ends of ribbons used to secure articles of clothing. They became larger and were eventually merely decorative ornaments, usually worn in pairs, attached to clothing or hats. Also, small decorative dress ornaments worn in suites. PAGE **40**.

Aigrette. A jeweled ornament in the stylized shape of feathers or serving as a holder for feathers. Usually worn in the hair or on a hat. PAGE **42**.

Archaeological jewelry. A nineteenth-century style that drew its inspiration from jewelry found at archaeological sites in Italy. PAGE **35**.

Bandeau. A narrow decorative band encircling the forehead. PAGE **56**.

Baroque pearl. A large pearl of irregular shape. PAGE **26**.

Bezel. The upper part of an ornamented finger ring. A decorative element formed from the same metal as the hoop encircling the finger, or the rim that holds stones, pearls, and cameos, etc., in a ring. Also the rim holding stones, rock crystal, and glass, etc., in such decorative items as watches. PAGE **37**.

Bulla. A hollow pendant, sometimes containing scent or an amulet, of Etruscan origin later adopted by the Romans. PAGE **38**.

Cabochon. An unfaceted stone with a highly polished, domed surface. PAGE **4**.

Chalcedony. A cryptocrystalline variety of quartz that includes agate, carnelian, and chrysoprase. PAGE **28**.

Champlevé enameling. A technique in which a metal is gouged out in a decorative pattern of troughs or cells, which are then filled with enamel. After firing, the enamel is polished down to the level of the top of the metal leaving a smooth, decorated surface. PAGE **36**.

Chaplet. A decorative ornament worn around the head. Also, a short rosary. PAGE **52**.

Châtelaine. A type of daytime jewelry hung from a belt, consisting of a hookplate with a number of chains. Household items such as keys, watches, needle cases, and seals were attached to the loose end of each chain. PAGE **87**.

Chrysocolla. A bluish-green stone sometimes confused with turquoise. PAGE **62**.

Cloisonné enameling. A technique in which thin, flat metal ribbons are bent into closed shapes called *cloisons*. The *cloisons* are affixed to a metal base in a decorative pattern and filled with enamel. After firing, the enamel is polished down to the top surface of the *cloisons*. PAGE **29**.

Collet. A band of metal encircling a stone and holding it in place in a setting. PAGE **26**.

Commesso. Carved hardstones, gold, and sometimes enamel, combined to create an image in relief. PAGE **29**.

En ronde bosse. The technique of enameling a raised or round figure. PAGE **82**.

Enseigne. A badge worn on the hat. Originating as humble signs of pilgrimage, these later evolved into more ornate decorations. PAGE **64**.

Faience. A ground quartz composition covered with a glaze made in ancient Egypt in colors sometimes imitating those of semiprecious stones. PAGE **7**.

Ferronnière. A ribbon or cord wrapped around the forehead and decorated with a jewel. PAGE **15**.

Fibula. An ancient brooch made in a form similar to that of a safety pin. PAGE **25**.

Filigree. Wire bent or twisted into a decorative pattern, soldered to a metal base or left as openwork. PAGE **11**.

Fillet. A decorative ornament worn around the head, often in the form of a wreath of leaves. PAGE **53**.

Foil. A thin sheet of colored metal placed under a stone to enhance its appearance or to create the illusion and color of a more precious gemstone. PAGE **16**.

Pomander. A pierced container that can be filled with a scented substance. Also, the ball of scent itself. PAGE **40**.

Repoussé. A technique in which the pattern on the front of a piece of metal is created by hammering or punching it from the back. PAGE **25**.

Rivière. A necklace of matched graduated gems set in simple mounts and linked together with no decoration. PAGE **87**.

Sardonyx. A variety of layered agate with brown and white bands used for cameos. PAGE **33**.

Scarab. An Egyptian amulet in the shape of a dung beetle. PAGE **102**.

Granulation. A decoration of tiny, round grains soldered to a metal surface, both usually made of gold. The Etruscan method, in which the solder was invisible, was not rediscovered until the 20th century. PAGE **11**.

Jacinth. A yellow-red to red-brown variety of zircon. PAGE **49**.

Lazo. The Spanish name for an openwork bow-knot shaped brooch set with gemstones. PAGE **49**.

Morse. An ecclesiatical clasp, which originated in the Middle Ages, used for fastening a cope. PAGE **79**.

Naoratna. A talismanic piece of jewelry made with nine specific gemstones. PAGE **98**.

Opus interrasile. A style of pierced decoration made by cutting an intricate pattern into a sheet of metal, usually gold. PAGE **66**.

Parure. A suite of matched jewelery containing a number of pieces, such as a necklace, diadem, earrings, bracelets, brooch. A set of just a few items is called a demi-parure. PAGE **24**.

Pinchbeck. An alloy of copper and zinc intended to imitate gold. PAGE **87**.

Plasma. A green subvariety of chalcedony. PAGE **4**.

Plique à jour. An enameling technique in which the enamel is contained in an openwork pattern of metal with no backing. The resulting piece is transparent, resembling a miniature stained-glass window. PAGE **85**.

Sévigné. The French name for an openwork bow-knot shaped brooch set with gemstones. Named after Madame de Sévigné, the seventeenth-century French court figure and writer of letters. PAGE **49**.

Signet ring. A finger ring with a seal. PAGE **101**.

Strapwork. A decorative pattern, usually enameled, resembling the interlacing of curved straps. PAGE **101**.

Table cut. One of the earliest types of gem cutting in which the top of an octahedral (eight-sided) crystal, one of the natural crystal forms of a diamond, is removed, creating a "table." PAGE **15**.

Wesekh. An Egyptian collar composed of many strands of colored beads. PAGE **9**.

List of Illustrations

PAGES 58–59. *Venus and Cupid*
Lorenzo Lotto (Venetian, ca. 1480–1556)
Oil on canvas
Purchase, Mrs. Charles Wrightsman Gift, 1986, 1986.138

PAGES 60–61. *Madame Paul Darras* (Henriette Oudiette)
Pierre Auguste Renoir (French, 1841–1919)
Oil on canvas
Gift of Margaret Seligman Lewisohn, in memory of her husband,
    Sam A. Lewisohn, and of her sister-in-law, Adele Lewisohn Lehman,
    1951, 51.200

Earrings
Greek, late 4th century B.C.
Gold
Harris Brisbane Dick Fund, 1937, 37.11.9–10

Earrings
Byzantine, 6th–7th century
Gold, sapphires, and pearls
Gift of J. Pierpont Morgan, 1917, 17.190.145,146

Earrings
Langobardic, end of 6th–1st half 7th century
Gold and turquoise-colored glass beads
Purchase, 1895, 95.15.124,125

Pair of Royal Earrings
Indian, ca. 1st century B.C.
Gold
Gift of The Kronos Collections, 1981, 1981.398.3,4

Earrings
Moroccan, 17th–18th century
Gold, rubies, emeralds, and enamel
Gift of Marguerite McBey, 1981, 1981.5.16–17

Earring
Egyptian, Dynasty 18
Gold, lapis lazuli
Gift of Helen Miller Gould, 1910, 10.130.1540

PAGES 62–63. *Whistle*
Mexican (Maya), 7th–9th century
Painted ceramic
The Michael C. Rockefeller Memorial Collection, Bequest of
    Nelson A. Rockefeller, 1979, 1979.206.953

Earplug Frontal
Peruvian (Mochica), 1st–3rd century
The Michael C. Rockefeller Memorial Collection, Purchase,
    Nelson A. Rockefeller Gift, 1968, 1978.412.206

Vessel
Mexican (Maya), 8th century
Painted ceramic .
The Michael C. Rockefeller Memorial Collection, Purchase,
    Nelson A. Rockefeller Gift, 1968, 1978.412.206

Ear Ornaments
Peruvian (Mochica), 3rd–6th century
Gold; stone and shell inlay
Gift and Bequest of Alice K. Bache, 1966 and 1977, 66.196.40–41

PAGES 64–65. *Hat Badge: Entombment of Christ*
French (Paris), ca. 1400–1410
Ronde bosse and basse taille enamel on gold and diamonds
Gift of J. Pierpont Morgan, 1917, 17.190.913

Hat Badge. Saint John the Evangelist with Lamb
Italian (Florence), ca. 1475
Gold, enamel, and jewels
Gift of J. Pierpont Morgan, 1917, 17.190.923

Portrait of a Man
Quentin Massys (Flemish, 1465/66–1530)
Tempera and oil on wood
The Friedsam Collection, Bequest of Michael Friedsam, 1931,
    32.100.49

PAGES 66–67. *Pendant: Cross*
German, third quarter of 16th century
Gold, enamel, and diamonds
The Friedsam Collection, Bequest of Michael Friedsam, 1931,
    32.100.306

Male Figure
Nigeria (Court of Benin), 17th century
Brass
Gift of Mr. and Mrs. Klaus G. Perls, 1991, 1991.17.32

Necklace
Byzantine, Constantinople?, mid-6th–mid-7th century
Gold
Gift of J. Pierpont Morgan, 1917, 17.190.151

PAGES 68–69. *Portrait of a Member of vom Rhein Family*
Conrad Faber von Creuznach (German, act. by 1524–d. 1552/53)
Oil and gold on wood
The Jack and Belle Linsky Collection, 1982, 1982.60.37

Rosary Bead
Flemish, ca. 1500–1525
Boxwood
Gift of J. Pierpont Morgan, 1917, 17.190.475

PAGES 70–71. *Jan, First Count of Egmond*
Master of Alkmaar (Dutch, act. ca. 1504)
Tempera and oil on canvas, transferred from wood
The Friedsam Collection, Bequest of Michael Friedsam, 1931,
    32.100.122

General Etienne-Maurice Gérard, Marshal of France
Jacques-Louis David (French, 1748–1825)
Oil on canvas
Purchase, Rogers and Fletcher Funds and Mary Wetmore Shively
    Bequest, in memory of her husband, Henry L. Shively, M.D.,
    by exchange, 1965, 65.14.5

PAGES 72–73. *Pectoral*
Byzantine, mid-6th century
Gold, niello
Gift of J. Pierpont Morgan, 1917, 17.190.1664

Necklace
Peruvian (Mochica), 3rd–6th century
Gold
Gift of Alice K. Bache, 1974, 1974.271.32

Fudō Myō-ō
Japanese, Heian Period (12th century)
Wood
The Harry G. C. Packard Collection of Asian Art, Gift of Harry G.
    C. Packard, and Purchase, Fletcher, Rogers, Harris Brisbane Dick,
    and Louis V. Bell Funds, Joseph Pulitzer Bequest, and
    The Annenberg Fund, Inc. Gift, 1975, 1975.268.163

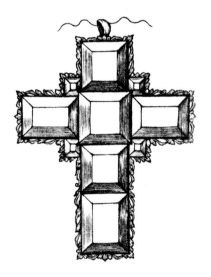

PAGES 74–75. *Judith with the Head of Holofernes*
Lucas Cranach the Elder (German, 1472–1553)
Tempera and oil on wood
Rogers Fund, 1911, 11.15

Reliquary Bust of Saint Yrieix
French, second quarter of 13th century
Silver-gilt, cabochons, crystal, and glass
Gift of J. Pierpont Morgan, 1917, 17.190.352

PAGES 76–77. *Madonna and Child with Angels*
Cosimo Rosselli (Florentine, 1439–1507)
Tempera on wood
The Friedsam Collection, Bequest of Michael Friedsam, 1931,
    32.100.84

Clasp
Workshop of Nicholas of Verdun (Mosan, ca. 1200)
Gilt bronze
The Cloisters Collection, 1947, 47.101.48

Fibula
Etruscan, 7th century B.C.
Gold
Purchase by subscription, 1895, 95.15.198

Oval Brooch
Viking, 10th century
Cast bronze with gilding
Purchase, Fletcher Fund and Bequest of Gwynne M. Andrews,
    by exchange, 1982, 1982.323.1

PAGES 78–79. *The Annunciation*
Hans Memling (Flemish, act. ca. 1465–d. 1494)
Oil on panel, transferred to canvas
Robert Lehman Collection, 1975, 1975.1.113

Morse
Italian (Tuscany), first half of 14th century
Copper-gilt and opaque and translucent enamel
Gift of Georges and Edna Seligmann, in memory of his father, the art
    collector Simon Seligmann, and his brother, René, 1979, 1979.498.2

PAGES 80–81. *Portrait of a Man and a Woman at a Casement*
Fra Filippo Lippi (Florentine, ca. 1406–d. 69)
Tempera on wood
Marquand Collection, Gift of Henry G. Marquand, 1889, 89.15.19

Nono (Mademoiselle Lebasque)
Henri Matisse (French. 1869–1954)
Oil on canvas
Bequest of Adelaide Milton de Groot (1876–1967), 1967, 67.187.83

Brooch
Attributed to Maison Rouvenat (French, ca. 1868)
Gold, enamel, and diamonds
Bequest of Xenophon Leonidas Mavroidi, in memory of Mary L.
    Mavroidi, 1946, 47.99

PAGES 82–83. *Christ Blessing, Surrounded by a Donor and His Family*
    (triptych)
Attributed to Ludger tom Ring, the Younger (German, 1522–84)
Tempera and oil on wood
Gift of J. Pierpont Morgan, 1917, 17.190.13–15

Saint Catherine of Alexandria
French (Paris, ca. 1400–1410
Gold, enamel, pearls, and precious gems
Gift of J. Pierpont Morgan, 1917, 17.190.905

PAGES 84–85. *Portrait of a Woman*
Rembrandt van Rijn (Dutch, 1606–69)
Oil on canvas
Bequest of Mrs. H. O. Havemeyer, 1929, H. O. Havemeyer
    Collection, 29.100.4

Lorgnette and Chain
René Lalique (French, 1860–1945)
Gold, enamel, diamonds, jade, and glass
Gift of Lettice L. Phelps Stokes, 1965, 65.154a–b

Louis Gueymard as Robert le Diable
Jean Désiré Gustave Courbet (French, 1819–77)
Oil on canvas
Gift of Elizabeth Milbank Anderson, 1919, 19.84

PAGES 86–87. *Madame Jacques-Louis Leblanc* (Françoise Poncelle)
Jean-Auguste-Dominique Ingres (French, 1780–1867)
Oil on canvas
Catharine Lorillard Wolfe Collection, Wolfe Fund, 1918, 19.77.2

Watch and Châtelaine
Movement signed: V. Blanck à Regensburg
Probably South German, third quarter of 18th century
Carnelian, gold, and gemstone
The Collection of Giovanni P. Morosini, presented by his daughter
    Giulia, 1932, 32.75.33

Watch
Movement by Josias Goullons (French, active ca. 1640–63)
Case and dial: enamel on gold
Gift of J. Pierpont Morgan, 1917, 17.190.1627

PAGES 88–89. *Gold Mounts*
Avaric, 6th–8th centuries
Gold
Gift of J. Pierpont Morgan, 1917,
    17.190.1673,1678,1683,1686,1697,1698

Girdle
Byzantine, late 6th–early 7th century
Gold
Gift of J. Pierpont Morgan, 1917, 17.190.147

Cowrie Girdle
Egyptian, from the Lahun Treasure, 18th century B.C.
Gold, carnelian, and green feldspar
Purchase, Rogers Fund and Henry Walters Gift, 1916, 16.1.5

Katharina Merian
Attributed to Hans Brosamer (German, act. by 1536–d. 1552?)
Oil and gold on wood
The Jack and Belle Linsky Collection, 1982, 1982.60.38

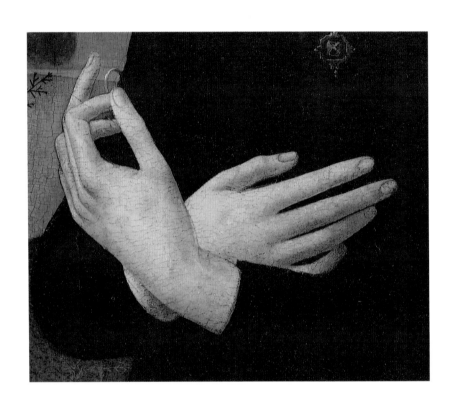

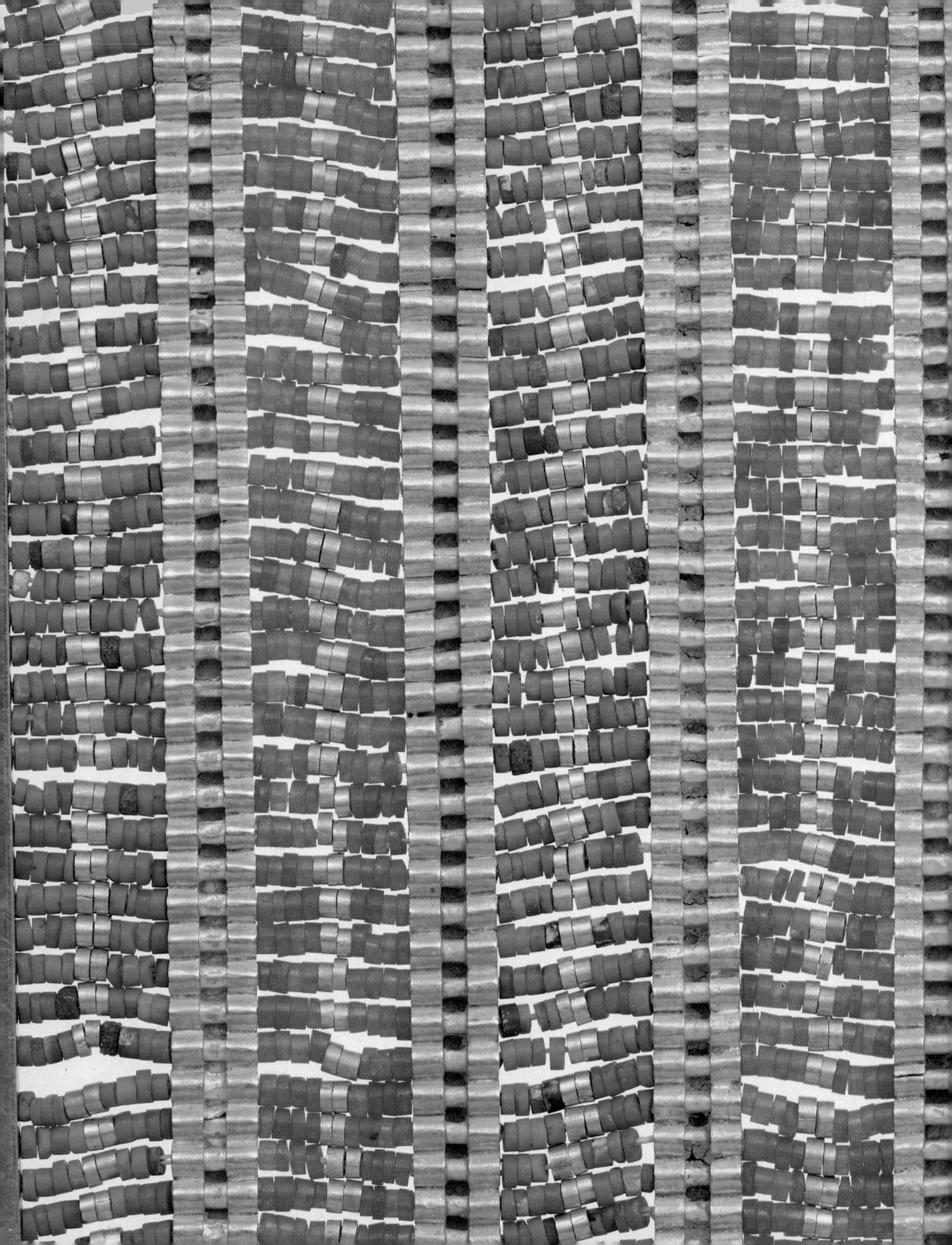